UNCAGE
THE LION

UNCAGE THE *Lion*

RELEASING THE POWER OF THE BIBLE TODAY

Editor: Becky Totterdell

Contributors: Peter Broadbent, Clive Calver, Steve Chilcraft,
Stephen Gaukroger, Peter Meadows, Nick Mercer,
Becky Totterdell

Design: Adept Design

Picture research, cartoons, graphics: Simon Jenkins

Acknowledgements

We are grateful to the following agencies and photographers for the use of their photographs.

Adrian Neilson/Scripture Union p50
Cephas Picture Library pp24, 118 , 120
David Simson pp26, 83
Gordon Gray/Scripture Union pp40, 56, 70, 77, 107, 115
Greenpeace Communications p22
Hutchison Library p116
Jesus Fellowship p20 (right)
John Rylands University Library of Manchester p81
Keston College p108
March for Jesus p119
Michael Holford p102 (top)
Mike Goldwater/Network p52 (right), 95
Paul Popper pp14, 52 (left), 92, 100
Press Association p64
QA Photo Library p12
Sonia Halliday Photographs pp48, 86
Stephen Butler/Reflexions p113
The Tank Museum, Bovington p102 (bottom)
Zefa Picture Library pp9, 18 (both), 20 (left), 33, 61, 89, 97 (both)

First published 1990 by Scripture Union, 130 City Road, London EC1V 2NJ
and Spring Harvest, 7 Cherwell Road, Heathfield, East Sussex TN21 8JT.
ISBN 0 86201 659 2

Also published by ANZEA Publishers, 3-5 Richmond Road, Homebush West, NSW 2140, Australia.
ISBN 85892-450-1

British Library Cataloguing in Publication Data
Uncage the lion: releasing the power of the Bible today.
   I. Totterdell, Becky
   220, 20
   ISBN 086201-659-2

Colour reproduction by J Film Process, Bangkok.

Printed and bound in England by Ebenezer Baylis & Son Limited, The Trinity Press, Worcester and London.

CONTENTS

INTRODUCTION

The Bible is still the world's best-seller. But it gets very mixed receptions. On the one hand there are all those nice white presentation copies which stay in their pristine condition, untouched, on living-room shelves. On the other, there are the tattered old copies which have been read, reread, memorised and prized above freedom and even life itself.

People who are hungry to hear and know God find his power released into their lives as they accept and apply the teaching of his word, the Bible. *Uncage the Lion* is designed to help *you* discover the power that is locked in your Bible, whether it is still 'good as new' or well-thumbed and dog-eared. The further you delve into the Bible the more you will discover its power: power to bring you closer to God and to understand what he asks of you.

In *Uncage the Lion* you will find:

● **Background information** about four major elements that go to make up the Bible: doctrine, history, Gospels and prophecy. There are also many **guidelines for how to apply the Bible's teaching** in the world of the twentieth century. Maps, charts, colour photographs and cartoons bring it all to life.

● **Eight Bible studies for groups.** These studies will help any small group take the topics further, become more familiar with the Bible itself and explore together the implications for them of the Bible's teaching.

To get the very most out of the group studies, make sure you obtain a copy of the **video** which has been made especially to link in with them. For each group study it provides eight to ten minutes of thought-provoking, stimulating material to lead the group into discussion. (At the back of this book there is an order form for the video.)

● Some remarkable **stories from around the world**. These show how the power of the Bible has broken into the lives of ordinary people as they have read it and allowed it to challenge them.

If we believe the Bible really does give us the truth about life we must blow the dust off it, open ourselves to what God has to say to us through it, and set about the task of reading, understanding, and applying it. As the saying goes, 'Bibles that are falling apart are generally read by people who aren't!'

DISCOVERING DOCTRINE

What exactly do we believe? And why do we
believe what we do?

WHAT IS DOCTRINE?

The gathered teaching of the Bible

Christian doctrines summarise the Bible's teaching, drawing together what it says about:

● God
● Humanity
● The world
● Salvation

and many other subjects linked with these.

Teaching on any one subject is scattered throughout the Bible, so working out Christian doctrines can feel like trying to put together seven jigsaw puzzles when the pieces have been jumbled in one box! Our ordered, twentieth-century minds prefer a more analytical, western approach. Couldn't God have put each bit of teaching in a separate section labelled 'church', 'evangelism', 'what happens when we die', and so on?

Perhaps he could have, but God chose instead to give us the Bible through the work of ordinary people who had their own styles of writing and whose thought patterns were those of the time and culture in which they lived.

The styles vary a great deal even within the Bible, as it was written by over forty authors during more than one thousand years in a wide range of political and geographical situations.

The Bible gives us a record of God's dealings with his people during this time. Sometimes it was appropriate for people to write letters about it, or poems, history books or accounts of what they had learnt about God — such as the ten commandments, which show us how God expects us to live. Together these provide a multitude of separate glimpses of God's character and activities. They are like the different types of flower in a garden: separately, each possesses its own beauty; together they make a coherent whole.

Revelation and inspiration

The Bible's teaching, from which we formulate Christian doctrine, claims to originate with God, not simply with those people who wrote it. When Paul wrote to Timothy, he said, 'All Scripture is God-breathed' (2 Timothy 3:16).

Two key words have traditionally been used by Christians to define the relationship between God and the Bible:

▶ **Revelation:** Taken from a Latin word which means 'removing a veil', this indicates that God has taken the initiative to make himself known to us. We cannot remove the veil of our ignorance about God ourselves — though this is what many religions around the world try to do. Instead, God has revealed himself to us in:
− General revelation: The order, beauty and vastness of creation, combined with humanity's moral sense, give us an idea of what the creator must be like.
− Special revelation: God gives us precise information about himself in the words of the Bible and, supremely, in the person of Jesus Christ, his Son.

► **Inspiration:** By this we understand that God has breathed his word through writers who acted as his spokesmen. God didn't use them as dictating machines, though, obliterating their personalities. Rather, 'men spoke from God as they were carried along by the Holy Spirit' (2 Peter 1:21). Their literary style, vocabulary and culture remained their own.

Because the Bible claims to be the revealed and inspired word of God, it also claims a third thing:

► **Authority:** God's words carry God's authority. Because of who he is we are wise to believe what he says and to act on those beliefs!

'The dual authorship of Scripture is an important truth to be carefully guarded. On the one hand, **God** spoke, revealing the truth and preserving the human authors from error, yet without violating their personality. On the other hand, **men** spoke, using their own faculties freely, yet without distorting the divine message.' *(John Stott, **Understanding the Bible**. London: Scripture Union, 1972)*

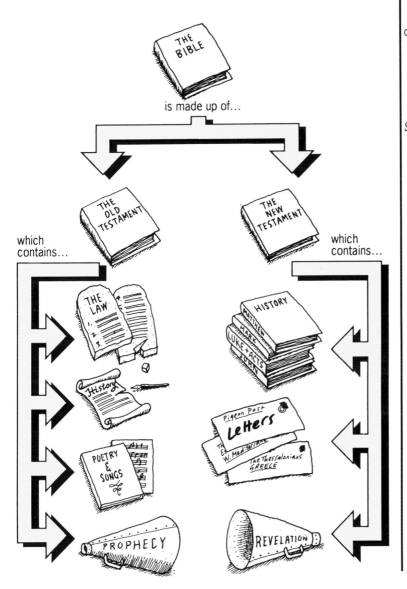

is made up of...

which contains...

which contains...

WHY IS DOCTRINE IMPORTANT?

Foundations and building blocks of the Christian life

There were two building contractors, each after the same nice plot of land on the Kent coast. One was smart. He got in there and started building his 'luxury executive homes' before the other could say 'Timetable'. The other was smarter. He looked up British Rail's development plans and saw that the rail route to the Chunnel would plough right into that patch of land. So he bought a nice plot in Essex, instead.

It is never enough to build our Christian lives on the strength of an experience we have had or on what other people have told us. We need to take time to check out the facts. The teaching the Bible gives is like the local searches and development plans any developer worth his salt would study carefully before deciding where to start digging: What actually happened when I became a Christian? What is the Christian faith really all about? What does God expect of me now? What does the Bible say about the future and the implications for the present?

In western society people build their lives largely on experience. Whether something is right or true depends, they say, on circumstances. Each person should do what is 'right for him', depending on his background and experience. That sounds fine – until you realise that we wouldn't even peel a banana on that basis! 'You feel like using dynamite to peel your banana? Well, go ahead. I'm sure that will be fine.' We certainly wouldn't build a house on the strength of what 'feels right for me'. You are quite free to build your three-bedroomed semi out of macaroni, but I don't suppose your wife and children will thank you for it after one or two April showers!

Some Christians don't stop to think what sort of foundations they are building on in their Christian lives, nor whether they are going about it in the right way with the right materials.

'Far more momentous than the choice even of a life-work or of a life-partner is the choice about life itself. Which road are we going to travel? On which foundation are we going to build? (*John Stott, **Christian Counter-Culture**. Leicester: IVP. 1979*)

The Channel Tunnel under construction. A person's Christian faith can withstand the pressures of life when it is built on solid doctrine.

Christian doctrine helps us to:

► Think right

Your mind matters! Jesus said, 'Love the Lord your God with all your heart and with all your soul and with all your mind' (Matthew 22:37). In other words, we are to think 'Christianly'. We can only do this if we understand the truth of what we believe. God has something to say about every area of life – war, abortion, sex, money, leisure, work. Doctrines explain what it is that God has to say and how he wants us to respond.

► Evaluate beliefs

Today, many world religions compete with the Christian faith. Only if we are aware of the distinctives of Christianity can we honour God by defending and expressing the truth.

Christians can themselves drift into error. Cults and sects, fresh ideas, new opinions and philosophies have challenged the church throughout its history. Charles Spurgeon, the nineteenth-century Baptist preacher, recommended using a straight stick to measure the crookedness of another. Doctrine is that 'straight stick'.

'England has two books, the Bible and Shakespeare. England made Shakespeare but the Bible made England.'
(Victor Hugo)

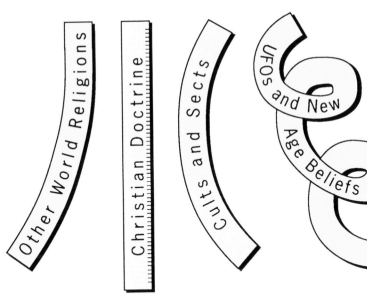

► Know God

If we want to get to know someone, we seize all the bits of knowledge about them that come our way and try to piece them together. What are her interests? What are her likes and dislikes? Knowing the right things will help us do the right things. Is it going to be *Black Magic* or a creme egg? A Count Dracula horror movie or *The Sound of Music*?

We get to know God by finding out about him through the teaching of the Bible. Calvin said that Jesus comes to us 'clothed in his gospel'. We can't separate knowing him from knowing the truths the Bible reveals about him.

'Loyalty to (Jesus) inevitably involves commitment to the truths about him. And conversely, carelessness or indifference concerning these biblical doctrines is a form of disloyalty to his name and unconcern for his honour.'
(Bruce Milne, *Know the Truth*. Leicester: IVP, 1982)

13

What we believe affects our whole way of life. The Nazi beliefs of the 1930s had a massive impact on the world, plunging millions into war. What effects will our beliefs have?

► Live right

The Aztecs of Mexico Valley thought that the sun was god and that it wanted human sacrifices. At the height of the Aztec civilisation about 20,000 people died each year because of this belief. The Bible shows us not only who God really is but also what he expects of us in daily living. Human sacrifice is not on his agenda!

'Getting doctrine right is the key to getting everything else right ... at every point right living begins with right thinking.'
(Bruce Milne, **Know the Truth**. Leicester: IVP, 1982)

The Bible tells us about:
● worship
● evangelism
● discipleship
● relationships
● work

► Share our faith

If we don't know what we believe, we won't be able to point other people to it, no matter how amazing our experiences may have been. Peter wrote, 'Always be prepared to give an answer to everyone who asks you to give the reason for the hope that you have' (1 Peter 3:15).

PERSONALLY SPEAKING

The Honesty Chain: Bible reading and social action

It is Zaire, 1977. As in many countries affected by economic chaos, corruption, like a sort of gangrene, has penetrated everywhere; hospitals, government offices, public services are all affected by the plague. Schools are the worst places for these unjust practices. To be enrolled or to pass exams students have to 'come to an arrangement' with their teachers. (You can imagine the sort of bribe that is often demanded from the women students.) To be well thought of the teachers themselves have to bribe their directors, who in their turn have to 'recommend' their school to the provincial inspector. It is easy to judge such a system, but those who are in the situation are overwhelmed by the pressure at the end of the month and driven to despair by galloping inflation and by the total lack of resources. Initially corruption seems the only way out.

At Easter 1976 a group of some twenty Scripture Union leaders met for a mini-camp at Kimpese. Earlier in the year God had spoken clearly to 130 members of a Bible training camp about the need to obey his word, not just to hear it. One morning, after a long period of personal prayer, a young Catholic teacher came to the meeting. With deep conviction he declared: 'As a Christian I can no longer take part in corruption. The Bible is clear about it. But I cannot tackle it on my own. We must face it together.'

His words opened up a whole new line of study, a new way of obeying. The Bible studies in the days that followed provided the biblical basis for action. How many times do the prophets speak on the subject! A definite project saw the light of day. Everyone there would form a kind of chain ... and, somebody added, 'It is Jesus who is the first link in the chain.' A Covenant and a list of members was prepared. Ngongo, the Christian teacher, became the second link as he signed. Mafuta, a Protestant teacher at the same school, was the third. Then each day more names were added. Each signature was a victory as everyone knew what it would mean in practice to sign: loss of employment, treatment could be refused at the hospital, children sent away from school.

In July of that year the teachers reported back on what had happened. Their first act had been to pin a notice on their classroom door: 'No corruption'. First they were laughed at, then they were threatened. After a bit they had to leave their homes and take refuge with the local pastor. Their lives had been saved but it was no easy experience. However, their example had upset the whole system of corruption in the school. A single shaft of light had destroyed the darkness itself.

Men, women and whole families suffered because they were willing to be honest in obeying the word of a just God. But this just God intervened, often in an astonishing manner, to look after his children.

The Honesty Chain has known its ups and downs. Each generation of Christians has to find concrete ways of facing its difficulties. Deep and serious Bible study was the origin of all this activity and the story is only worth telling if it challenges us about our desire to 'live the Bible'. What is our concept of the justice of God in our country? How could we show our loyalty to Jesus Christ? To what extent can we say that we believe in a new earth where justice reigns?

Danilo Gay

(Danilo Gay is the International Coordinator for Scripture Union Bible Ministries. He was a Scripture Union worker in Zaire during the time in which the Honesty Chain was started. This account was first published in the Scripture Union International magazine, *Catalyst*, No 8.)

DOCTRINE IN THE NEW TESTAMENT LETTERS

The New Testament letters (epistles) take Christian doctrines and relate them directly to real situations in particular churches. Subjects range from the uniqueness of Christ, his humanity and our justification by faith, to strategic instruction for times of persecution and how to live a Christian life in a pagan world.

Twenty-one of the New Testament's twenty-seven books are letters. Of these, Paul wrote thirteen. Seven others have named authors: James, Peter, John, Jude; but we do not know who wrote Hebrews.

Problems addressed by the letters

▶ **Conflict with Judaizers:** Jewish Christians were reluctant to loosen their Jewish customs and beliefs and some tried to make them binding on all Christians. Other Jews rejected the claim that Jesus was the Messiah and they opposed and attacked his followers.

▶ **False Teachers:** The early church was plagued with false teachers. Some believed that all physical, tangible things were evil and that only spiritual things were good. So they taught that truly spiritual people should 'punish' their bodies, avoiding marriage for instance and putting themselves through all kinds of exercises in self-denial.

Others thought that because we are saved by God's grace and not by anything we do, we no longer have to obey God's moral law. They led some Christians into gross immorality.

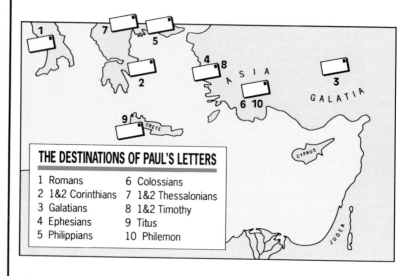

THE DESTINATIONS OF PAUL'S LETTERS

1 Romans	6 Colossians
2 1&2 Corinthians	7 1&2 Thessalonians
3 Galatians	8 1&2 Timothy
4 Ephesians	9 Titus
5 Philippians	10 Philemon

Others taught that salvation didn't come through repentance but through a process of enlightenment into special 'gnosis' or knowledge. They thought that God was so holy that he could have no part in human history. Jesus could not, therefore, have been God but only a created spirit who helped people climb the ladder of spiritual knowledge to God. They firmly dismissed the resurrection of Jesus and the future bodily resurrection of the Christian.

▶ **Conflict in the church:** Many young congregations faced difficulties and divisions. The immorality of society seeped into the life of the church. The threat of persecution proved a real pressure. There was also doctrinal confusion and uncertainty.

Paul's letters

Paul's letters make up nearly one third of the entire New Testament. There are three things to remember when reading his letters:

▶ **One half of a conversation:** Paul's letters are often replies to ones he had received, either from individuals or from churches, asking his advice about specific problems. Reading his correspondence is rather like hearing only one half of a telephone conversation. Sometimes we're not absolutely sure what the problem was and why it was a particular issue.

For example, in 1 Corinthians 15:29 Paul mentions the custom of baptising 'on behalf of the dead', as part of his proof of the resurrection of Jesus. The argument would have meant something to the church members at Corinth, but it is not so easy for us to follow because we don't know what that custom was all about.

▶ **Not organised Christian doctrine:** Because Paul was answering specific questions, he does not set out to give an organised presentation of Christian doctrine. That's not really surprising. If we wanted to know how to mend a fuse we wouldn't expect the person we asked for help to give us a three hour lecture on the properties of electricity! Hopefully, he would tell us only as much as we needed to know in order to get on and mend the fuse!

So, for example, we can't expect to find 'the doctrine of the church' fully explained in Ephesians, or 'the doctrine of grace' fully set out in Romans, although these subjects are major concerns of those letters.

'The writings which make up our New Testament arose out of very practical needs. It is not a cosy book of armchair religion. It was born out of the struggles and pressures in the lives of real people in the real world.'
(Chris Wright, **User's Guide to the Bible.** Tring: Lion Publishing, 1984)

▶ **Not all Paul's thinking:** Paul doesn't give all his thinking on one subject when answering a particular question. If we told one person we admired Margaret Thatcher, he might think we would vote Conservative at the next election. If it came out in conversation with someone else that we buy only recycled paper, always take our bottles to the bottle bank and grow all our own vegetables, she would guess we're voting Green. If we talk to someone else about our role as shop steward at work, he might assume we'll vote Labour. Paul gave help that was appropriate only to the church he was writing to, so we have to piece together all of these 'clues' before we can come to conclusions about his thinking.

For example, his teaching on what part women should play in worship is scattered throughout his letters. In 1 Timothy 2:8 – 15 and 1 Corinthians 14:33 – 36 it seems at first sight that Paul does not allow women to take any part in public worship. But 1 Corinthians 11:5 indicates that they did play a full part. It also seems that Paul benefitted greatly from the ministry of Priscilla, whom he described as a fellow worker (Romans 16:3) and was happy for her to teach Apollos more fully about the Christian faith (Acts 18:24 – 26). Paul's famous teaching about the equality of all people in Christ must also be taken into account when trying to decide what he thought about the role of women in the church: 'There is neither Jew nor Greek, slave nor free, male nor female, for you are all one in Christ Jesus' (Galatians 3:28).

Paul's letters speak to our world just as much as to the world of the first century AD. The appeal of the ancient theatre at Ephesus, continues in the modern world of theatres, cinemas and television.

FOR GROUPS:

HOW FIRM ARE YOUR FOUNDATIONS?

SHARE:

Share together a time in your life when your Christian faith was shaken – perhaps by a tragedy, by general stress and pressure, by doubts, or because of something else. What helped you keep hold of your faith during that time?

READ: Matthew 7:24 – 27.

EXPLORE: 1 Building the foundations

If we are to build substantial, lasting Christian lives, we need to be sure our foundations are rock solid and will support us when the world is throwing its worst at us.

● The two basic foundations of the Christian life are:
– commitment to Jesus himself (see 1 Corinthians 3:10 – 13; 1 Peter 2:4 – 6);
– an understanding of Jesus' teaching, given in the Gospels and explained more fully in the New Testament letters (see Ephesians 2:20; 2 Timothy 1:13 – 14; Hebrews 5:11 – 6:3).

Why is each vital to living the Christian life?

● Do you feel you should know more about either? If so, talk together about how you could find out more.

EXPLORE: 2 Living the life

● **Read what Jesus had to say about:**
▶ being different (Matthew 5:13 – 16)
▶ personal relationships (Matthew 5:27 – 32)
▶ truthfulness and reliability (Matthew 5:33 – 37)
▶ love for enemies and rivals (Matthew 5:43 – 44)
▶ giving (Matthew 6:1 – 4)
▶ fasting (Matthew 6:16 – 18)
▶ love of luxuries and money (Matthew 6:19 – 21,24)
▶ anxiety (Matthew 6:25 – 27,32 – 34)
▶ a judgemental attitude (Matthew 7:3 – 5)
▶ persistence in prayer (Matthew 7:7 – 12)

● Which of these teachings challenges you most? Share it with the group and talk about ways in which you might put it into practice this week. Be specific. Pray together for each other and for the help of the Holy Spirit in living out Jesus' teaching.

CAN CHRISTIAN DOCTRINE CHANGE?

Christian doctrines are drawn from the teaching of the Bible. The Bible's teaching never changes but there is always the possibility of our understanding of it being improved. At different times in the history of the church, existing understandings (doctrines) of the Bible's teaching have been challenged and refined.

▶ **Justification by faith:** Martin Luther, the sixteenth-century Reformer, challenged the doctrine of merit which was taught then by the Roman Catholic church. It was in opposing this that he clarified the doctrine of justification by faith alone through the grace of Christ alone.

While Sue of London is baptised in a tin drum, baby Christopher undergoes a formal Greek Orthodox infant baptism. Differences of doctrine can make a vast difference in how we practise our faith.

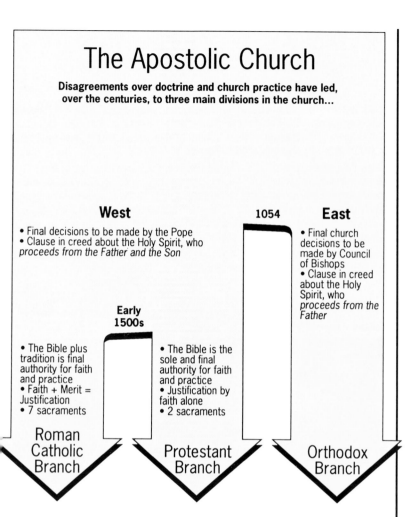

The Apostolic Church

Disagreements over doctrine and church practice have led, over the centuries, to three main divisions in the church...

West   1054   **East**

- Final decisions to be made by the Pope
- Clause in creed about the Holy Spirit, who *proceeds from the Father and the Son*

- Final church decisions to be made by Council of Bishops
- Clause in creed about the Holy Spirit, who *proceeds from the Father*

Early 1500s

- The Bible plus tradition is final authority for faith and practice
- Faith + Merit = Justification
- 7 sacraments

- The Bible is the sole and final authority for faith and practice
- Justification by faith alone
- 2 sacraments

Roman Catholic Branch

Protestant Branch

Orthodox Branch

▶ **'The last things':** The doctrine of 'the last things' – what exactly will happen at the end of time – has undergone considerable revision throughout church history. Revelation 20:1 – 6 speaks of a period of a thousand years during which believers will reign with Christ in victory. Many of the early church Fathers, such as Tertullian, Papias and Irenaeus, understood this literally. From the fourth century to the Middle Ages the period was taken symbolically. Since then some sections of the church have again taken it literally.

So, while we can have every confidence that the Bible's teaching is true, and remains so for all time, the Christian church finds that from time to time its understanding of that teaching is revised. All Protestant churches, however, are in agreement on all the major doctrines – the trinity, the lordship of Christ, the fallenness of humanity, salvation by faith through grace, the final authority of the Bible, the church and the kingdom of God. Different denominations differ to varying degrees over what are sometimes called 'secondary issues', such as infant baptism and church structure.

'In things essential – unity, in things doubtful – liberty, in all things – charity.'
(Richard Baxter)

HOW RELEVANT IS DOCTRINE TO TODAY'S ISSUES?

It all began with a barbecue, a group of friends and neighbours having a good time together. With everyone arriving more or less at the same time the cooking was a bit rushed and some hamburgers were rather under-done. But some people like their meat that way.

A few days later, Helen fell ill with what seemed to be a rather bad case of 'flu. But it turned out to be toxoplasmosis, an infection sometimes caught from under-cooked meat. Normally the infection is no more serious than very bad 'flu. But Helen is pregnant. Her GP has told her there is a strong possibility the baby will be born with some handicap but, as Helen is only twelve weeks pregnant, there would be no problem about an abortion.

Helen and her husband are Christians and know that many Christians are opposed to abortion. Up till now it has been a theoretical argument for them; they never expected to have to make such a decision themselves.

What should they do?

(Adapted from Martyn Eden and Ernest Lucas, **Being Transformed**. Basingstoke: Marshall Pickering. 1988.)

'This prevalent anti-doctrine spirit is a major departure from the Christian instincts of earlier ages and its roots go deep into contemporary western culture. In the face of the tremendous challenges and opportunities facing the church in the final decades of the twentieth century this dismissal of doctrines, in my judgement, is nothing short of a recipe for disaster.'
*(Bruce Milne, **Know the Truth**. Leicester: IVP, 1982)*

Greenpeace protesters project a message for the world onto the *Ark Royal*. Nuclear weapons were unknown in the time of the Bible, and yet the Bible lays down valuable guidelines in helping us to think about the issue.

Carol is finding her elderly mother increasingly difficult to look after. She is almost totally dependent on Carol for being washed, dressed and fed. And now she is beginning to forget where she is and even who Carol is. Carol already has her hands full looking after her three children and feels her mother is just more than she can cope with.

Should she try to get her into an old people's home?

Sue and Roger have just come back from their house group meeting. It ended in disarray after a 'heated discussion' on vegetarianism and animal rights. Sue is vowing never to buy meat again; Roger says she's over-reacting to what one person said about 'factory farming' and that it is quite all right for Christians to eat meat, especially when they don't have a say in how it is produced. **Should Christians be vegetarian?**

Many of the exact problems we face today were not known to the people who lived in the first century, so the New Testament teaches nothing directly about them. But it does give us a variety of principles, some applied in detail to the situations of those Christians. We can take these principles and apply them to our own situations.

For example, Helen and her husband would find that the Bible has something to say about the origins, nature and character of life. Carol would find that it has things to say about suffering and about caring for each other. Sue and Roger would find that it also speaks about the relationship of humankind to the rest of creation.

The Bible will rarely give us an 'off-the-shelf' answer. Normally we will need to take time to pray about the decision we have to make, to ask for insight from the Holy Spirit and to look for advice and support from other Christians.

'You've got to live in God's world, God's way.'
(Roger Forster)

Principles to look up
With the help of a Bible dictionary or concordance, explore the topics listed below under each issue. Then decide what principles are being taught and how they might relate to the two issues.

Care of the elderly:
► the purpose of life
► the value of life
► the body of Christ

Animal rights and vegetarianism:
► humankind's task on earth
► the image of God in humankind
► freedom in Christ

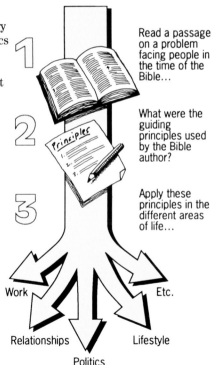

Read a passage on a problem facing people in the time of the Bible...

What were the guiding principles used by the Bible author?

Apply these principles in the different areas of life...

Work

Relationships

Politics

Lifestyle

Etc.

'If we have the Word but not the spirit, we'll dry up. If we have the Spirit but not the Word, we'll blow up. If we have the Word and the Spirit, we'll grow up.'

UNDERSTANDING THE NEW TESTAMENT'S TEACHING

How can we be sure that we have understood the teaching of the New Testament properly? There are four 'rules' that will help:

Rule number 1

'A text can never be expected to mean to us what it could never have meant to its author or readers.'

For example, in Philippians 4:13 Paul says, 'I can do everything through him who gives me strength.' Some Christians have taken this as a promise that God will help them achieve anything to which they put their minds. As Brian Abshire writes, 'While this may seem valid on the surface, a moment's reflection will reveal that it cannot mean this. If the verse really means that Christians can do 'everything', why don't Christians leap over tall buildings in a single bound, run faster than a speeding bullet or be more powerful than a steaming locomotive? . . . The meaning must be restricted somehow. Even so, many Christians have interpreted this verse to mean that they can do all sorts of things for which they were either ungifted, unprepared or unsuited.' (Brian Abshire, **Get More From Your Bible**. London: Scripture Union, 1988.)

When we look more closely at the text it becomes clear that Paul's emphasis is more on the 'can' than the 'everything'. He is affirming that despite the obstacles to his mission to the Gentiles (including that of being in prison) he is confident that God *will* enable him to carry out that mission.

Christians in the western world are immersed in a pagan culture. Adverts, movies, instant credit, glamour . . . We need to allow the Bible to challenge every aspect of modern life.

Rule number 2

'When we share a specific life situation with those addressed in the New Testament, God's word to us will be the same as it was to his people of that time.'

In other words, when we share the same context the message applies now just as much as it did then. For example, in 1 Corinthians 6:1 – 8 Paul rebukes two Christians for taking their dispute to be judged by a pagan judge in the local market place. They should have resolved it within the church fellowship instead. Or, if the worst came to the worst, 'why not rather be wronged?' asks Paul. The point of the passage doesn't change if the judge happens to be a Christian; the point is that Christians should not be taking each other to court.

It is not legitimate to say, on the strength of this passage alone, that a Christian should never go to court but should always take the alternative of 'being wronged'. This is because the *specific* situation would be different: the dispute might not always be between two Christians.

Rule number 3

'We must distinguish between teaching given in the New Testament for all time, and teaching that was given only for a specific, cultural situation.'

Most of the time we do make a distinction between these things, but often unconsciously and under the influence of our culture. For example, which of these commands do you regard as applicable only to the first century and which do you think should be binding on all Christians today?

● 'I want men everywhere to lift up holy hands in prayer' (1 Timothy 2:8).
● 'I also want women to dress modestly, with decency and propriety, not with braided hair or gold or pearls or expensive clothes' (1 Timothy 2:9).
● 'It is good for a man not to marry' (1 Corinthians 7:1).
● 'No widow may be put on the list of widows [to receive financial help] unless she is over sixty, has been faithful to her husband, and is well known for her good deeds' (1 Timothy 5:10).
● 'Stop drinking only water, and use a little wine because of your stomach and your frequent illnesses' (1 Timothy 5:23).
● 'It is disgraceful for a woman to speak in church' (1 Corinthians 14:35).
● 'Greet one another with a holy kiss' (2 Corinthians 13:12).

Our answers as to which are important for all people will largely reflect the cultural and religious traditions in which we have been brought up.

How can we avoid being unconscious victims of our cultural and church traditions? Gordon Fee and Douglas Stuart give us five clues:

'What is truth?'
(Pilate)

1 Distinguish between those truths which are basic to the gospel message (such as sin and redemption) and those which are secondary to it (such as drinking wine, speaking in tongues).

2 Distinguish between practices which the New Testament sees as matters of morality (such as drunkenness, idolatry, greed) and those which it does not (such as foot-washing, being unmarried, women teaching in the church).

3 Distinguish between those matters on which the New Testament always takes the same line (such as homosexuality, personal non-retaliation) and those where it varies (such as women's ministry in the church, being wealthy).

4 Distinguish between places where the New Testament is laying down a principle and where it is applying a principle. For example, in 1 Corinthians 11:2 – 16 Paul seems to be teaching the principle that nothing, including flouting social custom, should detract from the glory we give to God in worship. It seems that, within the passage, he is also applying this principle with regard to the social conventions of his day.

5 Be loving towards those Christians whose views differ from yours! We need to listen to each other and be prepared to accept that our interpretation may, just possibly, be wrong!

(Adapted from Fee and Stuart, **How to read the Bible for all its worth**. London: Scripture Union. 1983)

The unique power of the Bible is that it still speaks to us today. As we read it, the Bible helps us to make sense of life and to live as God intended us to.

Rule number 4

'Start by taking a New Testament passage or verse at its face value, but then go on to compare that with what the rest of the New Testament, and the Bible as a whole, teaches on that subject.'

For example, in James 2:14, 17 we find: 'What good is it, my brothers, if a man claims to have faith but has no deeds? Can such faith save him? . . . faith by itself, if it is not accompanied by action, is dead.'

Reading this at face value we might think that we have to earn our salvation by good deeds, as well as having faith in Christ's death for us. But we need to compare this with other teaching on the subject. For example, in Ephesians 2:8 – 9 Paul writes: 'For it is by grace you have been saved, through faith . . . not by works, so that no-one can boast.' We can then think more carefully about what Paul and James each had in mind when they spoke of 'faith' and 'works'.

WHAT ABOUT ABORTION?

SHARE:

The subject of abortion usually raises strong feelings. Some people are quick to condemn the action without really thinking of the people involved. So, before looking at the Bible's teaching, list as many reasons as you can for someone deciding to have an abortion. Put yourself in their shoes and try to see the situation from their perspective.

EXPLORE:

The Bible does not seem to say anything directly about abortion. It does give four principles, though, which relate to the decision.

1   Life is a gift from God.
2   God regards the unborn baby as an individual.
3   Fulfilment is not the result of being free of trouble.
4   Human beings are created for a relationship with God.

Look up the following verses. Which principles can be derived from which verses?

▶ Psalm 139:13 – 16

▶ Psalm 127:3

▶ Exodus 21:22 – 23

▶ Jeremiah 1:4 – 5

▶ Luke 1:39 – 45

▶ Philippians 2:3 – 8

▶ Romans 8:31 – 32

▶ 1 Timothy 2:4 – 6

DISCUSS:

On the basis of your study, how would you counsel (a) a Christian (b) a non-Christian who was thinking of having an abortion?

Pray together for anyone you know who is in this situation or suffering as a result of having an abortion and plan practical action to help her.

We will look at two basic doctrines of the Christian faith: the doctrine of God and the doctrine of the church. Each is formulated by drawing together teaching found in many different passages of the Bible.

GOD

The Bible does not try to give one single definition of God. Nor does it attempt to prove that God exists – it simply assumes the fact to be true. But it does tell us many things about him. Together, these make up our doctrine of God.

God: Who he is

The Bible nowhere gives a clear statement that God is a trinity – three persons but one being. The Christian doctrine of the trinity was developed from five strands of evidence drawn from the Bible:

● There is only one God (see Deuteronomy 6:4; Isaiah 45:22). The Jews of the Old Testament believed this and Jesus confirmed it (see Mark 12:29 – 32).

● Salvation comes from a three-fold source: God the Father, Jesus Christ and the Holy Spirit (see Ephesians 1:3 – 14).

● The disciples, who were Jews and believed in only one God, worshipped Jesus as God (see John 1:1; 20:26 – 29).

● The Holy Spirit is a person: he teaches Christians (John 16:12 – 14), helps us pray (Romans 8:26), encourages us (Acts 9:31), shares fellowship with us (2 Corinthians 13:14), is grieved by our wrongdoing (Ephesians 4:30).

● The Father, the Son and the Holy Spirit are three separate persons: the Father is not the Son or the Spirit, the Spirit is not the Son (see John 3:16 – 17; 16:7; 2 Corinthians 13:14).

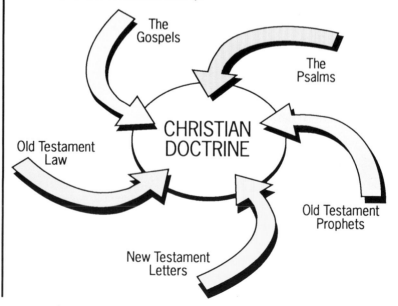

The Gospels

The Psalms

Old Testament Law

CHRISTIAN DOCTRINE

Old Testament Prophets

New Testament Letters

God: What he is like

Christian doctrine pulls together three sorts of teaching about God to describe what he is like:

● **His nature:** He is Spirit, he does not have a physical form; he is personal, not a force; he is eternal, he has never not existed and will never cease to exist; he is perfect, totally free from sin; he is transcendent (far beyond us) and immanent (close to us).

● **His attributes:** These things characterise God: omnipotence – he is all-powerful; omniscience – he knows everything; omnipresence – he is everywhere; glory; goodness; wisdom; love; grace; mercy; patience; holiness; righteousness; justice; faithfulness.

● **His actions:** Creation: he has created everything that exists. Providence: he directs all that happens in the world. Redemption: he has acted in Christ to redeem fallen humanity.

THE CHURCH

Throughout history God's aim has been to bring people into a relationship of love and trust with himself. Such a relationship is always dependent on God making the first move and it is maintained by God's grace.

Faith, law and covenant have always been the main elements in the relationship between God and his people. The Jews demonstrated faith in the only way open to them: by keeping the law and offering sacrifices. They lived in anticipation of the work of Christ (see Hebrews 11:39 – 40).

Christ's death was the ultimate sacrifice for sin and so freed God's people from the ceremonial law of the old covenant. The church is still subject to God's moral law though (see Hebrews 8:10), while not being dependent on it for salvation. This is the main distinction between the former people of God and the community founded on the day of Pentecost.

All God's people, from every age and culture, make up the church of Christ. When the church is complete (Romans 11:25 – 27) Jesus will return and the 'bride' will be united with the 'bridegroom' (Revelation 21:1 – 4). There will be a great celebration (Revelation 19:6 – 9) and God's eternal purpose will be complete. The church will enjoy uninterrupted fellowship with her Lord and will reign with him for ever.

Images of the church

The doctrine of the church is drawn from many images given in the Bible. It is described as:

● **The people of God**
(1 Peter 2:9; Titus 2:14):

► Separate from the world

► Called to belong to God

● **The body of Christ**
(1 Corinthians 12:12,27; Romans 12:4 – 5; Ephesians 2:20 – 22).

► With various gifts

► Mutually dependent

► Under Christ's leadership

● **The bride of Christ**
(Ephesians 5:27; Revelation 19:7; Hosea 1:2; 3:1 – 2)
▶ United with Christ
▶ Beautiful
▶ In a love relationship with Christ

● **The building of God**
(1 Corinthians 3:9 – 10; Ephesians 2:20 – 22; 1 Peter 2:4 – 6)
▶ Founded on Jesus
▶ Still being built
▶ A spiritual, not physical, building

● **The family of God**
(Ephesians 2:19; 1 Timothy 3:15)
▶ Sharing together
▶ God as its father

● **The branches of the vine**
(John 15:1 – 11; 1 Corinthians 3:6 – 8)
▶ Rooted and abiding in Christ
▶ Bearing fruit
▶ Being disciplined or 'pruned'

● **The flock of God**
(Hebrews 13:20 – 21; John 10:7 – 18; 1 Peter 2:25; 5:4; Acts 20:28)
▶ Jesus is its chief shepherd
▶ Dependent on God
▶ Liable to attack from outside

The church in action

The book of Acts and the New Testament letters give us a fairly clear idea of what different local churches were doing. Paul's letters are particularly helpful because they point out things that had gone wrong in some of the churches and what should have been happening instead. When we pull all these passages together we can draw up a picture of what we should find churches doing today:

● **Worshipping God**
(1 Corinthians 14:26)
▶ Through song, prayer, the Bible, spiritual gifts.

● **Proclaiming the gospel**
(Acts 1:18; 4:33)
▶ Witnessing to Jesus in the power of the Holy Spirit.

● **Teaching**
(Acts 2:42; Titus 2:1 – 2)
▶ Explaining the Bible's teaching so that everyone can understand it and act on it.

● **Praying**
(Acts 4:31; Ephesians 6:18)
▶ Praying together on behalf of others, waiting on God, engaging in spiritual warfare.

● **Baptising**
(Matthew 28:19; Acts 16:33)
▶ Symbolising that the believer has died, with Christ, to sin, and has been raised with him to new life.

● **Breaking bread**
(Acts 2:42; 1 Corinthians 11:17 – 34)
▶ Remembering together, with bread and wine, the death of Jesus.

● **Supporting those in need**
(Acts 6:1 – 3; James 2:15 – 16)
▶ Practical support for those in need.

● **Giving**
(1 Corinthians 16:1 – 3)
▶ Giving generous financial help.

● **Mission**
(Acts 13:4 – 5; 19:8 – 10)
▶ Sending missionaries and encouraging other fellowships.

● **Sharing fellowship**
(John 13:34 – 35; 2 Thessalonians 1:3 ; 1 Peter 4:9)
▶ Encouraging and supporting one another in living the Christian life.

'If a man is not familiar with the Bible, he has suffered a loss which he had better make all possible haste to correct.'
(Theodore Roosevelt)

30

● **Leadership**
(Romans 12:4 – 8; Ephesians
4:11 – 12; 1 Timothy 3:1 – 10)
► The church needs people to
minister to it and lead it: elders,
deacons, pastors, teachers and
others.

● **Discipling**
(1 Timothy 4:6; Hebrews 12:5 – 11)
► Correcting errors; rebuking sin;
challenging to change.

● **Using gifts**
(1 Corinthians 12:7 – 11)
► Every member is gifted by God
and has a contribution to make to
the local church.

● **Suffering**
(Revelation 2:3, 9 – 13; 3:8 – 10)
► Suffering for the sake of Christ
and in defence of the gospel's truth,
power and purity.

PERSONALLY SPEAKING

A Bible for eight pounds of potatoes

Miltos Anghelatos was brought up in a Greek Orthodox family on the island of Corfu. He writes, 'At a very young age I began to search for God. I used to sit with a friend on the marble steps of our school building. Looking up at the skies we used to ponder "What about God?" ' He had no Bible to help him find the answer. As he grew older, he gave up his search for God but set himself wholeheartedly to study. 'Day and night I probed into human wisdom, with only a short pause for food and few hours of sleep.' But none of this satisfied him. By the winter of 1942, when he was twenty, he was in despair.

One day, when he was reading a novel by the Russian author, Leo Tolstoy, he noticed some words on the title page that puzzled him. 'Unless an ear of wheat falls to the ground and dies, it remains only a single seed. But if it dies it produces many seeds. John 12:24.' He was intrigued by these words, but had no idea who John was or what the numbers 12 and 24 meant. So he asked his English teacher, who told him they came from the Bible. He asked his teacher what the Bible was. The teacher replied that the Bible was a book that people called missionaries had taken to the South Sea Islands, and when they had given this book to cannibals, the cannibals stopped eating people!

This made Miltos determined to get a Bible. He searched the whole town and eventually found one he could buy second-hand. The price was eight pounds of potatoes, a very high price in wartime, when food was scarce.

'It was about midday when I began reading the Bible and it was almost midnight when I put it down. The next day, sitting on the small hill behind our house, I sat there, with the Holy Book of God open in my hands.' For those first months he read for over ten hours a day. 'Nothing could withstand the light of this book of God. Ever clearer I saw how wretched I was. Snapshots showing scenes of hate, deceit, theft, embezzlement, which had so far orna-mented my life, were dragged to the surface. In no way could I excuse myself.'

Things came to crisis point the follow-ing January. 'At last I came to the end of my tether. That afternoon, like the magicians of old, I brought out the archives of the life I had led before I knew Christ, my books, my pictures, my writings, and threw them all on the fire. Then I knelt down. I did not say much. It was tears that gave me tongue. In shame and repentance I brought to the foot of the Cross of Christ the whole of my liabilities, all my sins which the Holy Spirit had brought to my memory. I felt in the very depths of my soul the joyful assurance that "the blood of Jesus Christ cleanseth you from all your sin." I had discovered the truth I was searching for. I did not find it in human wisdom but in the Gospel of my Lord Jesus Christ.'

(Miltos Anghelatos is the Director of Scripture Union in Greece. His story is told by Nigel Sylvester in *God's Word in a Young World*. London: Scripture Union, 1984.)

The city of Petra, stronghold of the Nabateans in about 300BC, seen through a crack in the rock. Why is it important to understand the Bible's history?

WHY BOTHER WITH HISTORY?

Hard on the heels of 'Trivial Pursuits', quiz books of 'Bible trivia' are now becoming popular: 'How many wives did King Solomon have? How did Eglon die? What was the fifth plague that God sent on Egypt?'

It's fun trying to answer the questions but is 'getting the right answers' the only reason for delving into Bible history? It doesn't seem to be of much practical use; knowing who Eglon was doesn't do a great deal for my Christian life! Some of the history recorded in the Bible is also pretty unsavoury. What are we to make of all the battles and the warlike way in which God is presented?

'History is important for without it we are at the mercy of whims. Memory is a data bank we use to evaluate our position and make decisions. With a biblical memory we have two thousand years of experience from which to make the off-the-cuff responses that are required each day in the life of faith.' (*Eugene Peterson, A Long Obedience in the Same Direction.* London: Marshall Pickering, 1989)

History is actually very important to each of us. We keep photo albums to remind us of family get-togethers and of what Jane looked like when she was three; we dust meticulously around the silver cup won at a sports event years ago; a scrapbook or two keeps a motley collection of receipts from cafes, tickets from museums and postcards to remind us of past holidays. We might even have stashed away somewhere a lock of hair from the baby's first haircut!

Our own history matters to us. It puts our lives in a context and helps us to understand ourselves better. It reminds us of the people who have been important to us in the past, or to whom we have been important. Looking back on our past can give us a sense of achievement or satisfaction. Keeping records of what has happened helps us to remember those events more accurately than we would if we had to rely only on our memory.

The same is true of Bible history. In particular, Bible history does three things for us:

● Bible history sets the context for today's church

The church did not suddenly appear on this earth as if it had dropped from another planet; it grew out of the Old Testament people of God. Bible history is the Christian's family history. In it we learn about past family members, discover the family's roots in Judaism and see what makes Christianity different from all other religions.

● Bible history helps us understand God better

Bible history is the story of how God has worked through and for the people we read about in it. By becoming involved in human life, God has shown us what he is like in very tangible, concrete ways. As we read the Old Testament histories we get a clear idea of God's character, his concerns and his plans for humanity.

● Bible history gives us firm grounds for trusting God today

For instance, Bible history shows that God keeps his promises, so we have good reason to trust and obey him today. It shows that the Christian faith is founded on fact and not on stories or wishful thinking. It shows that God's ultimate plan for all humanity — that of being brought into a relationship with him — is being worked out by him throughout all history, first through Old Testament Israel and now through the church.

WHAT IS BIBLE HISTORY ALL ABOUT?

Bible history on three 'levels'

The Bible records history on three levels. To understand its message we need to be aware of what these levels are and look out for them as we read it (see Fee and Stuart, **How to read the Bible for all its worth**).

▶ **The top level:** God's universal plan, worked out through his creation. Key elements of this are: the creation of the world; the fall of humanity; God's plan of redemption; Christ's incarnation, death and resurrection. This plan carries on into the present day and will be completed with Christ's second coming and the creation of a new heaven and a new earth.

▶ **The middle level:** How God works out that plan through the fortunes of his people: Israel and the church.

▶ **The bottom level:** All the individual narratives that make up the other two levels; the records of incidents in the lives of kings, prophets, apostles and ordinary people.

The recurring themes of Old Testament history

Like any good story, the story that comprises Old Testament history has a number of recurring themes. These tell us a great deal about the meaning of the events being recorded, and help to explain why the historians chose to record certain events and not others.

● **God acts on behalf of his people:**
▶ Supernaturally, as in the flood and the exodus (Genesis chapters 6 – 8; Exodus chapters 7 – 11; 13:7 – 14:31).
▶ Through circumstances, as with Joseph (Genesis 45:1 – 11) and Esther (Esther 3:12 – 4:14).
▶ In leadership, as with the Judges (Judges 2:10 – 19) and kings (1 Samuel 16:1 – 14).

● **God punishes sin and rebellion:**
► Of his people (Numbers 11:1 – 3; Joshua 7).
► Of leaders, as with Miriam and Aaron (Numbers 12), Moses (Numbers 20:1 – 13), Saul (1 Samuel 15).
► Of nations (Joshua 11:16 – 20; 1 Samuel 5; 2 Chronicles 20).

● **God is Lord of the whole earth:**
► In its creation (Genesis 1:1 – 2:3).
► In its preservation, as promised after the flood (Genesis 8:20 – 9:17).
► In setting limits to man's power in it, as with Pharaoh (Exodus 6:1 – 8).

● **God is present with his people:**
► In person, as Jacob and Moses discovered (Genesis 35:9 – 15; Exodus 3:1 – 12).
► In their places of worship: the tabernacle (Exodus 40:34 – 38) and the temple (1 Kings 8:1 – 30).
► When they are on the move (Joshua 1:1 – 9).

● **God promises a future Messiah:**
► His coming is prophesied: in the garden of Eden (Genesis 3:15); when Jacob blesses his son, Judah (Genesis 49:8 – 10); when Balaam prophesies about Moab (Numbers 24:15 – 19).
► His death is prefigured: when Abraham is called to sacrifice Isaac (Genesis 22:1 – 14); in the passover feast (Exodus 12:1 – 32); when Moses strikes the rock to bring out water (Exodus 17:1 – 7).
► The forgiveness bought by his death is anticipated in the sacrificial system (Leviticus 1:1 – 6:30).

● **God's word is given to his people:**
► In prophecy: directly to individuals, to Abraham for example (Genesis 17:1 – 8) or indirectly through prophets (see for example, 2 Kings 7:1 – 2, 20).
► In law: given to Moses (Exodus 19:16 – 20:17; 24:4 – 7).

● **God reveals his desire for pure worship**
► By giving instruction (Exodus 25 – 31; Deuteronomy 7:1 – 6).
► By exhortation to avoid idolatory and syncretism (Exodus 32:1 – 35; Deuteronomy 4:15 – 24; 2 Chronicles 28:22 – 27).
► By giving instructions on how to enhance worship by using the creative skills he has given (Exodus 35:30 – 36:5; 1 Chronicles 16).

THE BOOKS OF BIBLE HISTORY

Where do we find Bible history?

● **In the Old Testament:** The Jews of Jesus' day grouped the books of their scriptures, our Old Testament, into three sections: law, prophets and writings. The Christian church has grouped them slightly differently: law, history, wisdom, prophets. These categories are not exact, though. Genesis, grouped with the 'law' books, does not contain any laws but all five 'law' books do contain historical narrative. Similarly, the wisdom and prophetic books contain much material that relates to the social, politcal and cultural background in which they were written. The history element of the Old Testament is therefore found in several books, not just in those formally categorised as 'history'.

● **In the New Testament:** The Gospels and Acts carry on the story of God's dealings with his people, and with the whole world through the church's missionary work. The 'continuing history' is still written on three levels: God's ultimate plan for the whole world; his involvement with his people, the church; and the lives of the individuals who are caught up into these two bigger story lines.

THE JEWISH SCRIPTURES

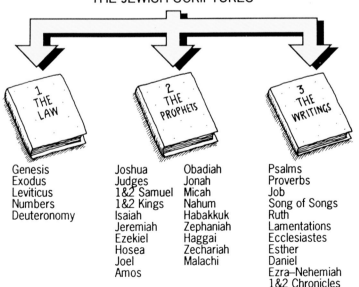

Genesis	Joshua	Obadiah	Psalms
Exodus	Judges	Jonah	Proverbs
Leviticus	1&2 Samuel	Micah	Job
Numbers	1&2 Kings	Nahum	Song of Songs
Deuteronomy	Isaiah	Habakkuk	Ruth
	Jeremiah	Zephaniah	Lamentations
	Ezekiel	Haggai	Ecclesiastes
	Hosea	Zechariah	Esther
	Joel	Malachi	Daniel
	Amos		Ezra–Nehemiah
			1&2 Chronicles

THE CHRISTIAN BIBLE

Law

5 Books:
- Genesis
- Exodus
- Leviticus

History

12 Books:
- Joshua
- Judges
- Ruth
- 1 Samuel
- 2 Samuel
- 1 Kings
- 2 Kings

Wisdom/Poetry

5 Books:
- Job
- Psalms
- Proverbs

Prophecy

17 Books:
- Isaiah
- Jeremiah
- Lamentations
- Ezekiel
- Daniel
- Hosea
- Joel
- Amos
- Obadiah
- Jonah
- Micah
- Nahum
- Habakkuk

History

5 Books:
- Matthew
- Mark
- Luke

Letters

21 Books:
- Romans
- 1 Corinth.
- 2 Corinth.
- Galatians
- Ephesians
- Philippians
- Colossians
- 1 Thess.
- 2 Thess.
- 1 Timothy
- 2 Timothy
- Titus
- Philemon

Prophecy

1 Book:
- Revelation

- Numbers
- Deuteronomy

- 1 Chronicles   • Esther
- 2 Chronicles
- Ezra
- Nehemiah

- Ecclesiastes
- Song of Songs

- Zephaniah
- Haggai
- Zechariah
- Malachi

- John
- Acts

- Hebrews   • Jude
- James
- 1 Peter
- 2 Peter
- 1 John
- 2 John
- 3 John

What period does Bible history cover?

● **Undated history** (sometimes called 'proto-history'): It will probably never be possible to put a date to the first events recorded in the Bible. What we can say is that Genesis chapters 1-11 cover a period up to about the year 2000 BC.

● **From the patriarchs to the settlement of Canaan:** The rest of Genesis, relating the lives of Abraham, Isaac, Jacob and Joseph; the story of the exodus and wilderness wanderings (Exodus, Leviticus, Numbers, Deuteronomy) and the settlement in the promised land (Joshua) takes Bible history up to about 1360 BC.

● **The period of the Judges:** The period of the Judges followed this, dating from about 1360 to 1050 BC.

● **From the monarchy to the fall of Samaria and Jerusalem:** Saul became Israel's first king in 1050 BC. The kingdom split in 930 BC, dividing into the kingdom of Israel, with Samaria as its capital, and the kingdom of Judah, with Jerusalem as its capital. Samaria fell to the Assyrians in 722 BC and Jerusalem was captured by the Babylonians in 586 BC. The books of Samuel, Kings and Chronicles record this period of history. It was probably towards the end of this time that Jonah's missionary trip to Nineveh took place and that Amos and Hosea were speaking out against injustice and corrupt worship.

History repeats itself. It has to. No-one listens.

STEVE TURNER

Pardon?

ANON.

Mount Hermon stands 30 miles south-west of Damascus. It would have been one of the last familiar landmarks that the exiles .from Israel and Judah passed as they were taken to Assyria and Babylon.

'The sweep of this sacred history is magnificent. Although it omits great areas of human civilisation which would feature prominently in any history of the world written by men, yet in principle and from God's point of view it tells the whole story of man from start to finish, from the beginning when 'God created the heavens and the earth' (Genesis 1:1) to the end when he will create 'a new heaven and a new earth' (Revelation 21:1).'
(John Stott, **Understanding the Bible***. London: Scripture Union, 1984)*

● **The exile:** Daniel was one of the captives taken to Babylon and his book relates subsequent events there and under Darius the Mede. The book of Esther records events that affected the Jewish community which had settled in Susa, the capital of Persia.

Isaiah, Jeremiah and Ezekiel were significant figures during this period, continuing to bring God's prophetic word to his people in their times of downfall and captivity. During the earlier period of exile Micah, Zephaniah, Nahum and Habbakuk were active, their prophetic roles being carried on in the latter stages of exile and return by Haggai, Zechariah, Obadiah, Joel and Malachi.

● **The return to Judah and the rebuilding of Jerusalem:** The first group of exiles returned to Jerusalem in 538 BC. The second came back with Ezra in 458 BC and the third with Nehemiah in 432 BC. The books of Ezra and Nehemiah give us accounts of how Jerusalem was rebuilt and worship was restored to the temple.

In 432 BC Nehemiah was recalled to the service of King Artaxerxes in Susa, Persia. He was able to return again to Jerusalem for a second period, the length of which is uncertain. After Nehemiah's accounts, the Old Testament's record of the history of God's people ceases.

● **The coming and ministry of the Messiah:** The Gospels take up the history of God's people again. They are accounts of the arrival, ministry, death and resurrection of the Messiah and records of his people's reaction to him.

● **The church age:** The book of Acts chronicles the growth and spread of the church − the New Testament people of God. The book of Revelation, generally regarded as a prophetic book, looks forward in 'history', painting a vast, impressionistic picture of the close of the age and the fulfilling of God's purposes for his creation.

HISTORY CONTINUES IN MISSION

A missionary people

Israel was designed to be something of an introduction agency. In biblical terms, it was to have a priestly function. It was to introduce God to the world by showing what God was like (1 Kings 8:41 – 43) and, as the nations around became attracted to its God, Israel was to introduce them to him. Isaiah speaks very clearly of God's intention to extend the covenant to all nations (see Isaiah 42:6; 49:6).

Jesus was the perfect embodiment of Israel. He was the perfect image of God ('He who has seen me has seen the father', John 14:9) so could show what God is like. Those who come to Jesus discover that they may approach God through him ('I am the way', John 14:6) and are brought into a living relationship with God.

As people continue to come to God through Christ the church grows and the history of God's people continues.

The early spread of Christianity

The book of Acts carries forward this history as it chronicles the missionary work of the early church:

► Acts 1:15:   120 disciples

► Acts 2:41:   3000 more are added

► Acts 4:4:   Many more join the church; the men alone now number 5000

► Acts 6:1,7:   The number of disciples increases rapidly

► Acts 8:1 – 4:   Persecution scatters the church; every Christian plays a part in evangelism

► Acts 9:31,35:   Churches are established throughout Palestine, with whole villages turning to Christ

► Acts 11:19 – 21:   Gentiles become Christians; the evangelisation of the nations begins

► Acts 16:5:   Growing churches are established in what is now Turkey

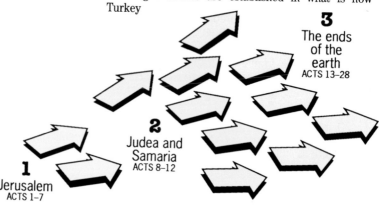

3
The ends
of the
earth
ACTS 13–28

2
Judea and
Samaria
ACTS 8–12

1
Jerusalem
ACTS 1–7

► Acts 16:10 – 11: Paul and his companions set off for Europe: more Gentiles become Christians

► Acts 21:20: James and the elders of the church in Jerusalem report that thousands of Jews are becoming Christians

According to Revelation 7:9 the eventual number of Christians will be uncountable!

Church growth and mission today

The nineteenth century was the great century of missions. At its close an urgent call went out to form a strategy for reaching the whole world with the gospel. More recently, the Lausanne Congresses on world evangelisation (1974 and 1989) have attracted huge numbers of evangelists, missionaries and church leaders concerned to find more effective ways to reach people with the gospel. The people of God still have much to do:

● 1,385,000,000 people in the world today know nothing about Christ, Christianity or the gospel.

● The Bible has yet to be translated into more than 800 major languages and nearly 3000 others.

Yet the church worldwide is growing at a rate of 1.7% each year; much of the current growth and impetus for mission is coming from Africa, the Middle East, Latin America, the Caribbean and Asia.

PERSONALLY SPEAKING

A street kid in Lima

Isaac Salcedo was born in a town in the mountains of Peru. But, at the age of seven, he ran away from home because of his drunken and violent father. After a few months, when he was nearly eight years old, he arrived in Lima – with great hopes. 'It seemed like heaven and I was sure I would get some help, but instead I was thrust into a world of evil.' Isaac became one of the thousands of runaway and abandoned children who live on the streets of Peru's capital city. 'The only refuge I found was the big vegetable market. At night I slept in a great mound of fruit boxes. My only food was the fruit they threw away.'

Before long, Isaac was part of a gang of street kids who taught him how to steal. When he was twelve the police caught up with him and put him in a reformatory. But he soon managed to escape and his life of crime continued. After killing a policeman who had started to beat him, Isaac fled to Ecaudor but was later sent back to Peru where he was arrested. Isaac was offered release on the condition that he would do military service. This he did but the discipline of the army did nothing to reform his lifestyle; he was frequently in jail.

Once, when Isaac was twenty-five and drunk, he went into a church, just for a rest. It turned out to be an evangelical church where the Gospel was being preached. The text used in the sermon was Luke 9:23, 'If anyone would come after me, he must deny himself, and take up his cross daily, and follow me.' This was a significant text for Isaac. It showed him that his life at that time was worthless before God and that he needed to change. There in the church he committed his life to Christ. The next day, although he was still drunk, he remembered what had happened the day before and three months later he confessed his faith and was baptized.

(Isaac is now a pastor in Peru and is on the staff of Scripture Union. His story is told by Michael Hews in Scripture Union's International magazine, *Catalyst*, No 8.)

REMEMBER WHAT GOD HAS DONE!

SHARE:

What has been one of the major turning-points in your life? How did it change you or your outlook on life?

READ:

Deuteronomy 4:32 – 40. Moses is speaking to the Hebrew people forty years after God had brought them out of Egypt. They are still in the wilderness but about to enter the Promised Land.

EXPLORE:

1 What did the events of the past reveal to the Hebrew people about God?

2 How might the people's awareness of who God was and of what he had done in the past affect:
▶ their view of the future?
▶ their day-to-day living in the present?

3 When you hear what God has done in other times or places, how do you feel?
(a) Depressed: God doesn't do things like that in my life.
(b) Indifferent: So what? I'm interested in the here and now.
(c) Sceptical: Of course, you must take it all with a pinch of salt.
(d) Excited: It all shows what a great God we have!
(e) Hopeful: What God can do in one situation he can do in another.
(f) Other:..
What makes you feel this way?

4 Think about the 'history' of your own relationship with God:
▶ Write down three things that God has done for you, or three occasions where he has been particularly significant in your life.
▶ How can these facts be an encouragement to you in your day-to-day Christian living?
▶ How do these facts encourage you about the future?
If you would like to, share some of these things with the group.

READ:

Romans 8:32 – 39. Pick out the things that Paul says God has done for us, and the effects those actions have on our present and our future. Pray together, thanking God for what he has done.
*(Adapted from John Grayston, **From God With Love: Serendipity Discipleship Series**. London: Scripture Union, 1986)*

It is a common assumption that the Bible, particularly the Old Testament, is full of inacuracies, contradictions and bias, perhaps excusable only if it is not supposed to be understood literally. While there are undoubtedly problem passages – places where the meaning is not at all clear or where the apparent reading seems to claim something impossible – the problems are not as frequent or as damaging as we may have been led to believe. The difficulties can be grouped into two main areas.

SELECTIVITY OF MATERIAL

The strongest attacks on the Bible have been aimed at the selectivity of its history. The *Concise Oxford Dictionary* defines history as a 'continuous methodical record of important or public events'. Critics point out that biblical history presents an unbalanced picture of the world, leaving out all reference to the great empires of Babylonia, Persia, Egypt, Greece and Rome except for those times when they impinge on the fortunes of Israel and Judah. Even when reporting events within the kingdoms of Israel and Judah, the material is not selected by the political criteria that a modern western historian would choose. Omri, for example, was one of Israel's most notable kings. His foreign policy was outstanding and he brought great stability and prosperity to the kingdom. Yet his reign is passed over in just six verses of 1 Kings 16. On the other hand, an entire book is devoted to the family life and fortunes of Ruth, a young widow who was not even an Israelite.

There are three points to note about the selectivity of Bible history:

Value-free history is not possible
It is now generally recognised that no one can write a 'value-free' history. At the least, a historian will come to his subject with his own presuppositions, experience and expectations. He is necessarily selective in the information he chooses to investigate, restricted by limitations of time, finance, knowledge and his own areas of special interest.

The Bible historians state their purpose
The clear purpose of the writers of Bible history was to declare the truth about God: his covenant love for his people and the response he required from them. Material was selected for its usefulness in illustrating this. Omri is therefore assessed on the basis of how he responded to God's claims on him, rather than on the success of his foreign policies. Similarly, Moses's struggles with Pharaoh to bring about the release of the Hebrew slaves are recorded with an eye to teaching future generations about the power of God, not the negotiating skills of Moses.

Because of its 'revelatory' nature, biblical history can be compared to prophecy. J A Motyer writes, 'Like prophecy, history in the Old Testament is a declaration from God about God.' And, 'It was a correct and deep perception that entitled the corpus of literature from Joshua to Kings "The Former Prophets" '(J A Motyer, **Old Testament History**, in Frank Gaebelein (ed), **The Expositor's Bible Commentary Vol I.** Grand Rapids: Zondervan, 1979).

The selectivity of the Bible historians does not mean their accounts are untrue

Biblical historical accounts are unusually frank about the shortcomings and failures of their national figures. They stand in stark contrast to the propagandist histories of surrounding nations of the time, Egypt and Assyria for instance. The historians allowed the people of Israel no hero except for God himself. Moses, the great leader who was said to have spoken with God face to face, is shown falling at the last hurdle and so is denied the opportunity to take God's people on into the promised land. We see King Solomon become world-famous for his wisdom and wealth, then read the historian's sad commentary: 'Solomon did evil in the eyes of the Lord; he did not follow the Lord completely' (1 Kings 11:6). Even Elijah, the formidable prophet who challenged kings to mend their ways, is shown frightened and depressed. Historical accuracy works to the advantage of the biblical writers: through all the failures and weakness of humanity, God is seen to be working out his purposes unerringly.

FACTUAL ACCURACY

▶ Did creation happen just in six days?
▶ Did Abraham really exist?
▶ What about the contradictions in figures given in parallel passages of Samuel and Chronicles?

Problems like these, relating to the factual accuracy of the Old Testament, can generally be solved by asking one or more of the following questions.

What type of literature is it?

When querying the scientific or historical accuracy of parts of the Old Testament, we need to check out the purpose and genre of the literature. Genesis chapters 1 to 11, for example, which speak of creation in six days and of Adam and Eve, were not written as a scientific textbook on creation or the origins of man. They are, rather, theological and philosophical tracts for the times, correcting contemporary false ideas about the nature of God, the world, and of humanity's role within it. Those chapters should therefore be read on their own terms; it is not legitimate to brand them as 'unscientific' and, consequently, 'inaccurate'.

What recording conventions are being followed?

● **Genealogies:** It has often been pointed out that the biblical genealogies are highly stylised and do not match up with information given elsewhere in the Bible. The genealogy in Matthew 1:1 – 17, for instance, includes the statement that 'Joram [was] the father of Uzziah'. This does not tally with the information given in 2 Kings 8:23 – 25; 11:2; 14:1,21. These verses make it clear that there were in fact three generations between Joram (also known as Jehoram) and Uzziah (also known as Azariah). The difference between the records in Matthew and Kings can be explained by taking into account the theological purpose of Matthew. He divides Old Testament history into three eras (Abraham to David; David to the exile; the exile to the coming of Jesus) and lists each as consisting of fourteen generations. The phrase 'A was the father of B' does not necessarily imply direct fatherhood. Matthew writes this stylised account in order to emphasise the perfection of God's plan for his people and of his timing in sending Christ. It was a convention understood by the Jewish readers for whom he wrote.

The same device has been used in the genealogy of Genesis 5, tracing the line of descent from Adam to Noah. If we take this to be a full, continuous list of generations, we must suppose that Adam appeared on earth some 1,947 years before Abraham, in about the year 4000 BC. It is impossible to reconcile this, however, with the external data of archaeology, which bear witness to the existence of civilizations many thousands of years before this date. Again, it should not be assumed that these genealogies are meant to be complete. The symmetry of their generations – ten from Adam to Noah (Genesis 5) and ten from Noah to Abraham (Genesis 15) – indicates otherwise. We also have evidence from other civilizations of the Ancient Near East that this was an accepted and understood convention. The Abydos King List in Egypt omits three entire groups of kings at three points in an otherwise continous series. A similar method was used by the compiler of the contemporaneous Sumerian King Lists.

● **Great ages:** The Bible attributes life-spans of hundreds of years to those who lived before the flood (Genesis 5). While this may reflect conditions in a world where the pre-flood climate was a much more hospitable one, it may simply be a further example of recording conventions. Long life-spans are also recorded for the pre-flood kings of Mesopotamia, varying from 18,600 years to 43,000 years! We know, however, that the kings they list were historical figures and lived for quite normal periods of time. It is therefore reasonable to suppose that Genesis 5 speaks about real people, but uses a convention whose purpose we have not yet discovered.

Archaeology can help bring the Bible to life. These excavations at Capernaum in Galilee reveal what was very probably Peter's house, which Jesus made his home after leaving Nazareth.

What can archaeology tell us?

'The purpose of biblical archaeology is to recover material remains of man's past, not to "prove" the accuracy or historicity of the Bible. Nevertheless it is important to note that Near Eastern archaeology has demonstrated the historical and geographical reliability of the Bible in many important areas... It is now known, for instance that, along with the Hittites, Hebrew scribes were the best historians in the entire Ancient Near East.' (E M Blaiklock and R K Harrison (eds), **The New International Dictionary of Biblical Archaeology.** Grand Rapids: Zondervan, 1983.)

The work of archaeologists and students of the literature of other Ancient Near Eastern peoples has been able to clear up many problems met by readers of the Bible. In particular, they confirm the accuracy of the biblical historians when writing about:

● **People:** Many figures who appear in biblical history, especially the kings of Israel and Judah, are also mentioned in the annals of the kings of neighbouring states.

● **Customs:** Excavations of places such as Mari and Nuzi in Mesopotamia serve to illustrate that the customary laws reflected in the patriarchal stories fit better into the framework of the social and legal practices of their day than into that of later Israel. Many of the customs mentioned in Genesis died out before 1000 BC. For example, at Nuzi it was the custom for a barren wife to purchase a slave girl in order to produce children for her husband. This accords well with the events of Genesis 16 concerning Sarah and Hagar. Similarly, parallels to customs surrounding inheritance (Genesis 15:3) and land transactions (Genesis 23) have been found in the course of archaeological research at these sites.

● **Places:** For example, the narratives concerning the lives of Abraham, Isaac and Jacob, which purport to relate to a period between 1900 and 1600 BC, mention a number of towns by name. After 1600 BC drastic changes took place in Palestine and large numbers of towns sprang up. Yet only the pre-1660 BC place names are mentioned in the patriarchal narratives.

For example: there is absolutely no mention of Skegness.

Thank goodness.

'As I have dealt with one apparent discrepancy after another and have studied the alleged contradictions between the biblical record and the evidence of linguistics, archaeology or science, my confidence in the trustworthiness of Scripture has been repeatedly verified and strengthened by the discovery that almost every problem in Scripture that has ever been discovered by man, from ancient times until now, has been dealt with in a completely satisfactory manner by the biblical text itself or else by objective archaeological information.'
(Gleason Archer, Encycopedia of Bible Difficulties. Grand Rapids: Zondervan, 1982.)

What do further textual and linguistic studies show?

The non-specialist Bible student can do much to resolve the tensions and problems he or she encounters in the text, simply by careful study of the text and by some reference to the works of biblical linguists. Gleason Archer, Professor of Semitic Studies at Trinity Evangelical Divinity School, Illinois, gives the following guidelines for solving Bible problems.

Some recommended procedures for dealing with Bible difficulties

1 Be fully persuaded in your own mind that an adequate explanation exists, even though you have not yet found it, just as an aerodynamic engineer trusts that there is an adequate explanation of how a bumble bee can fly, even though he has not yet figured it out. We can have complete confidence that the divine author of the Bible prevented the human authors from making mistakes as they wrote down the original manuscripts of the text.

2 The Bible is either the authoritative Word of God or the fallible words of men. There is no need to jettison the former belief (which was held by Jesus) simply because you encounter something you cannot understand or square with another passage. It might not be the Bible that is at fault, but your own understanding.

It is not always easy to identify biblical sites. Et-Tell, a mound of ruins, is in the right location for biblical Ai, the city destroyed by Joshua in the early stages of his conquest of Palestine. Yet excavations indicate that the last major city on this site was destroyed almost 1000 years before the time of the conquest.

3 Carefully study the context (paragraph, chapter, possibly even book) and framework of the verse in which the problem arises, until you gain some idea of what the verse is intended to mean within its own setting.

4 Commit yourself to discovering what the author meant by the words he used. Did he mean them to be taken literally or metaphorically? If literally, what exactly did he mean? Use a Hebrew or Greek dictionary to help you discover the exact meaning of the words.

5 Assume that parallel passages can be harmonised. That is, all the testimonies of the various witnesses are to be taken as trustworthy reports, though seen from different perspectives and with different interests, and that together they give a fuller understanding of the event than we would have simply from one of the sources.

6 Consult commentaries on the passage, along with Bible dictionaries and encyclopaedias.

7 Hebrew was written originally only in consonants; vowel signs were not added until a thousand years after the completion of the Old Testament canon. Many Bible difficulties result from a minor error on the part of a copyist in the transmission of the text. For example, it seems that the scribes copying the manuscripts sometimes misplaced the vowel signs in the Hebrew words, so producing different words. In other places, some similar-looking consonants were confused and the wrong ones written on the copy. The works of textual critics must be referred to in order to clear up these difficulties. Detailed commentaries on the book in which the problem occurs will usually explain the solutions they propose.

8 Whenever historical accounts of the Bible are called into question on the basis of alleged disagreement with the findings of archaelogy or the testimony of ancient non-Hebrew documents, remember that the Bible is itself an archaeological document of the highest calibre. It is simply crass bias for critics to hold that whenever a pagan record disagrees with the biblical account, it must be the Hebrew author that was in error. Pagan kings wrote self-commendatory propaganda, just as their modern counterparts do! No other ancient document from the period before Christ affords so many clear proofs of accuracy and integrity, even in its copies, as does the Old Testament.

(Adapted from Gleason Archer, **Encyclopedia of Bible Difficulties**. Grand Rapids: Zondervan, 1982.)

PERSONALLY SPEAKING

A Businessman builds on the Bible

Kurian is an Indian Christian aged sixty-two. I first met him in September last year. A well-educated and successful businessman working as an executive in industry in Bombay, he became involved with a group from his church who served as voluntary social workers at one of the city's overcrowded municipal hospitals but, as he read the New Testament, he was challenged by Jesus' declaration at Nazareth recorded in Luke 4:16-21, but also by the story of the sheep and the goats in Matthew 25:31-46. Soon he realised that God was asking more of him.

Kurian lived in a prestigious apartment block situated in the Marol district of Bombay near to a shanty town slum, housing some 5,000 people. The slum is populated by those who have migrated from the rural villages of India to the urban centres in the hopeless search for a livelihood. Kurian and his wife began to look for a way of becoming part of the life of these people and showing them something of Jesus.

In 1980, having spent a great deal of time in prayer, Kurian decided to take action. First, he invested his personal savings in a large piece of the scrap land which he had often viewed from his apartment window. Then, with the help of some friends, he slowly erected a school building for the children of the area. Built from second-hand materials he had been able to obtain from demolition sites around the city, the school now has around 150 pupils between three and six years of age. The project has been so successful that a second school was opened in 1988 in another slum area nearby. Most of the teaching staff were initially volunteers though an important emphasis of the work has been to train adults from the slum itself as teachers and so use the minimum of outside help. This policy means that quite apart from the obvious benefits to the children, the project also provides work and training for adults who would otherwise remain unemployed.

Three years ago Kurian decided to take early retirement in order to give his time fully to running and developing the school. The 'Marol Neighbourhood Project' now includes a clinic which gives inoculations and supplies simple medicines at very low cost and often completely free of charge. There is also a job creation scheme for women which teaches needlework and tailoring. In the near future it is also hoped to set up a job training project for men alongside one or two simple business schemes.

(Reported by Steve Chalke, Director of Oasis Trust, London.)

PERSONALLY SPEAKING

A piece of paper in the road

N Gnanaraja was converted in India at the age of seventeen through a piece of paper he found lying in the road. It was a page torn from an English Bible. He had been brought up in a Christian home but failure and frustration had caused him to deny the existence of God.

He took the page home and said to his family, 'If God was alive, he wouldn't allow this page to be torn from the Bible!' But his sister read out the verse at the top of the page: 'His boastings have wrought nothing.'

'This verse was a shock to me', Gnanaraja said later. 'I became restless and saw that unless I changed, I could not have peace.' So he knelt beside his bed and committed his life to Christ.'

(N Gnanaraja is the General Secretary of Scripture Union in India. His story is told by Nigel Sylvester in *God's Word in a Young World*, London: Scripture Union, 1984.)

THE NEW TESTAMENT'S VIEW OF HISTORY

In Ephesians 3:10-11 the apostle Paul gives a view of history that is radically different from that of the modern secular historian:

'[God's] intent was that now, through the church, the manifold wisdom of God should be made known to the rulers and authorities in the heavenly realms, according to his eternal purposes which he accomplished in Christ Jesus our Lord.'

Paul implies three things about world history:

▶ **It has a meaning:** Paul writes of God's 'eternal purposes' and 'intent'.

▶ **It is focused in the work of Jesus Christ:** he is the fulfilment of all human history.

▶ **Its meaning is revealed in the church:** The key to the ultimate significance of world history is not to be found by studying text books of battles, peace treaties and the rise and fall of empires, but among God's people; an astonishing claim! People will only discover the purpose of the world and its happenings if they look to the work of God in the church. John Stott writes:

'Secular history concentrates its attention on kings, queens and presidents, on politicians and generals, in fact on "VIPs". The Bible concentrates rather on a group it calls "the saints", often little people, insignificant people, unimportant people, who are however at the same time God's people and for that reason are both "unknown (to the world) and yet well-known to God."' (John Stott, **God's New Society: The Message of Ephesians**. Downers Grove: IVP. 1979.)

The Bible insists that there is a transcendent dimension to life on this earth. Human history, it claims, cannot be interpreted simply in terms of 'life under the sun' (Ecclesiastes 2:11,17). What, then, is the message of biblical history for us today?

News items often focus on the lives of rich, powerful VIPs. But the Bible has another focus. It reveals how God fulfils his purposes for the world through people who are often insignificant, poor and weak.

WHAT DOES BIBLE HISTORY TEACH US TODAY?

In his essay, *God and History*, James Montgomery Boice outlines five major doctrines that are taught through biblical history.

● **Creation:** There is a unity in the history of the human race.

► The Bible teaches that the human race is not an accidental part of the created order but is, rather, that most valuable part of creation for which the other parts were brought into existence. This has a number of implications. Firstly, humankind is set apart from the rest of the creation: people are not simply created elements on a par with molluscs, rocks and chimpanzees. Secondly, God remains distinct from humankind. Thirdly, God is distinct from the created world; the latter is not to be worshipped as if it were God. Fourthly, humankind is responsible under God for the stewardship of the planet.

► The human race is one: the Bible teaches the unity of the human race and that all human beings from all races are included in God's one purpose for the world. Recent attempts by historians to come up with a single 'key' to understanding world history have, however, brought very diverse results. It is simply not possible for a finite human being to produce a history of the world that is not finite and limited. The Bible, however, with its 'God's-eye view' of the world, claims to provide this ultimate framework for viewing history.

● **Providence:** God controls history.
The Bible teaches that, having created the world, God did not then abandon it but has been, and still is, intimately involved in guiding the course of its history. This takes us into one of the great mysteries of the Christian faith: the relationship between the eternal will of God and contrary human wills. While we cannot say exactly how that relationship works, we can say that each party has genuine freedom. As a result, human response to God's call either in obedience or disobedience is significant for the overall unfolding of history.

● **Revelation:** History has a pattern and goal, which God makes known to us.
It is only through the inspired writings of the Bible that we are let in on God's purposes for the world. The Bible's revelation of the world's history and purpose starts with the picture of mankind as first created. It was a state which did not last long. From its third chapter, the Bible can only tell the history of a fallen mankind. But this account has a driving purpose behind it: it looks forward to the coming of the 'second Adam', the perfect man, Jesus Christ, in whose hands lies the destiny of the entire human race. All of history from the creation of the world, the spreading out of the nations, the choosing of a special people, narrows down to the baby of an otherwise unknown Jewish girl. And from that fragile life, the whole course of the history of humankind spreads out again, with the church springing up and taking the news of the world's messiah to all corners of the earth. Only a God's-eye view could have produced this account, cutting across nations and centuries to trace the central thread of human history.

'Since the writing of history involves selection and interpretation of facts and since selection is always made at least in part on the basis of the subjective experience and judgment of the interpreter, it is actually impossible to write a purely objective history... The only way out of this problem is to receive an interpretation of history from outside history, as it were, from a being who perfectly understands history but who is above and beyond it and is therefore not affected by the distortions and prejudices that living and working in history introduce.'

(J M Boice, 'God and History' in Kenneth S Kantzer (ed), **Applying the Scriptures.** *Grand Rapids: Zondervan, 1987.)*

● **Redemption:** God acts redemptively in history.

The concept of redemption is fundamental to the good news of the world's messiah. The doctrine brings together the fact of sin and the fact of Jesus' death, in history, to save the sinner.

▶ Naturalistic and nonethical views of human history, which discard the concept of sin, do not do justice to the world as we know it. Some historians have seen the world's history as one of continuous, though fitful, 'progress'. But this idea cannot be sustained in the face of reality; whatever humankind tries to do is, sooner or later, marred by sin. Others have sought to show that the destructive element in mankind is contained only within institutions and can be eliminated by social restructuring or revolution. But the Bible reveals that the problem is deeply rooted in the nature of men and women. Only God's restructuring of human nature will be sufficient to change it decisively.

▶ It was to bring about this 'restructuring' that Christ came. His coming thus formed the pivotal point of all history. The most fundamental concern of mankind – his very nature – is at the heart of the Bible's account of history.

● **Judgment:** People are responsible for what they do or do not do within the flow of history.

The doctrine of God's final judgment at the end of history is a crucial one. It does not, however, imply that the meaning of history is only going to be disclosed at the end of it. It is the moment-by-moment decisions, choices and actions made by individuals throughout the world that weave human history. Each action or decision has its significance and will receive its judgment.

The Bible teaches that the important moment in history is **now**. History is like a Beethoven symphony: each note is of significance and is an indispensible part of the whole, although the work is not complete until the last note is played. In the small 'notes' of history as well as in the final return of Christ and the establishing of his kingdom, God's glory will be revealed. 'We envisage our history in the proper light, therefore, if we say that each generation, indeed each individual, exists for the glory of God.'

(Adapted from J M Boice, 'God and History' in Kenneth S Kantzer (ed), **Applying the Scriptures**. Grand Rapids: Zondervan. 1987.)

THE COVENANT AND THE LAW

Central to the message of the historical books of the Bible are the covenant which God made with Israel and the laws which he gave them.

The covenant

Covenants were well known in the Ancient Near East. They were legal agreements between mutually consenting partners. In reality, one partner was usually more powerful than the other; the stronger one would often be promising military protection in return for the loyalty and tribute of the weaker partner. Archaeology has provided us with examples of covenants from the Egyptians, Akkadians and Sumerians, dating as far back as 3000 BC.

The concept of covenant is central to God's dealings with his people. The essence of his covenant with Israel is contained in his promise: 'I will be your God and you shall be my people' (eg Genesis 17:7; Exodus 6:7). It is a covenant promise carried on into the New Testament (see 2 Corinthians 6:16 – 18; Revelation 21:3).

God established the covenant unilaterally, but it needed both sides to keep it. God promised to bless his people, spiritually and materially, in order that they could in turn be a blessing to the whole world. In return God's people were to love and obey him. Exactly how they were to do this was set out in the laws he gave them. Time and again, however, his people failed to keep the terms of the covenant and a consistent pattern emerged:

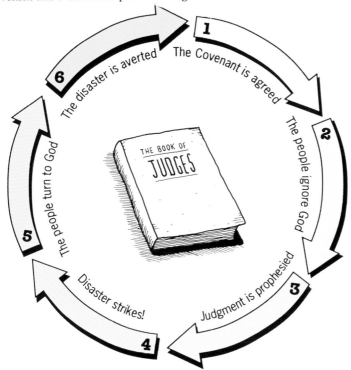

Eventually, Israel's persistent disobedience meant that she forfeited the benefits of the covenant, even to the extent of being taken away from the promised land and becoming 'not my people' (Hosea 1:8 – 10) in exile in a foreign country.

But God did not revoke his covenant. Its promises held good for all who would accept it by faith and live in accordance with its stipulations. There would always be a few, a remnant, who, through judgment, repentance and forgiveness, would enjoy the fulfilment of the covenant promises. The law of God would be written on their hearts. So Old Testament history pointed forward to the coming of the Messiah. His sacrificial death atoned for the sins of God's people under the old covenant and established the new with all future generations and peoples who would come to him in faith (1 Corinthians 11:23 – 26; Zechariah 2:10 – 11).

'Troubles are often the tools by which God fashions us for better things.'
(Henry Ward Beecher)

55

The Law

The laws given to Israel by God are set out in four fairly well-defined blocks:

▶ **The ten commandments:** These were basic to Israel's conduct (Exodus 20:1 – 17; Deuteronomy 5:6 – 21).

▶ **The book of the covenant:** This is the name given to a whole code of laws which show how God's covenant people should live. It shows how the basic laws of God given in the ten commandments are to be applied justly, lovingly and peaceably (Exodus 21 – 23).

▶ **The levitical law:** This expresses God's concern for holiness and purity. Most of the laws relate to the construction of the tabernacle, the consecration and ordination of priests, the offerings and sacrifices, rules of purity, holy days and vows. Blessings and curses are attached to this code: God promises that the people will be blessed if they keep the laws in it but warns that disaster will follow if they do not (Exodus 25 – 31; 35 – 40; Leviticus 1 – 27; Numbers 4 – 10).

▶ **The deuteronomic law:** This further explains and applies the laws of the book of the covenant in the light of Israel's new historical situation. The laws are given as Israel is about to enter the promised land and so relate to the settled lifestyle of an established nation (Deuteronomy 1 – 30).

'People need to be reminded more often than they need to be instructed.'
(Dr Johnson)

On Mt Sinai, one of the key events of the Old Testament took place. It was here that God spoke to Moses, giving to the people of Israel the Law that would help them live as *God's* people.

Fitting together 'law' and 'gospel'

Jesus was the mediator of a new covenant between God and humankind, a covenant which promised salvation 'by grace through faith', not salvation through keeping laws. So what role do God's laws play today? Are Christians meant to keep the Old Testament laws?

The law was actually never given as a way of salvation but as a way of life for those who were already in the community of God's people. It gave concrete examples of the way in which his people should live: showing what it meant in practice to be holy, just and loving, perfectly reflecting the character of God. Jesus restated the requirements of the Old Testament law in a new way in his sermon on the Mount (Matthew 5:1 – 12). The 'laws' he gave there, like those given on Mount Sinai to Moses, were again addressed to those already in a covenant relationship with God – in this case to the disciples. They show how the disciples, and all future believers, should live as God's covenant people.

The law cannot *make* us holy, just and loving if we are not already that by nature. In fact, it can only make us aware of how far short we fall of its requirements. As such it prepares us for the remedy offered in the gospel. It becomes our 'tutor to bring us to Christ' (Galatians 3:24). It is he who has the power to give us a new nature, one that is holy, just and loving. What is more, he gives us the Holy Spirit to empower us to live in a way that is in accordance with our new nature.

'The real job of every moral teacher is to keep on bringing us back, time after time, to the old simple principles which we are all so anxious not to see.'
*(C S Lewis, **Mere Christianity**. London: Collins, 1975)*

How do we apply Old Testament law today?

Jesus perfectly fulfilled the Old Testament law – he kept all its requirements – but he did not abolish it. What is more, he seemed to expect his followers to keep it too (Matthew 5:17 – 20). But the laws of the Old Testament are very specifically applied to particular times, people and places. How do we know which elements of those laws still apply to 'new covenant' people and which do not? Here are three guidelines:

● Keep those that are restated in the New Testament. The ten commandments, for example, are restated in various ways (see Matthew 5:21 – 37). Jesus summarised the entire 'law and the prophets' in just two commands: love God and love your neighbour as yourself (see Matthew 22:37 – 40).

Hmm. Where's the bit about double-yellow lines?

● Discard those revoked by the New Testament. For example, Peter writes of *the church* as 'a chosen people, a holy nation, a people belonging to God' (1 Peter 2:9). We can assume from this that the civil laws of the Old Testament, devised for a particular nation, no longer apply to the New Testament people of God. In the same way, the book of Hebrews makes it clear that the ceremonial laws have been superceded by the priestly and sacrificial work of Christ.

● Look for principles that may be applied to today's situations:

▶ Is a *reason* given with the law? (See, for example, Deuteronomy 24:21 – 22.)

▶ Did *later believers* derive a principle from an earlier law? (See, for example, Deuteronomy 25:4 and 1 Corinthians 9:1 – 11.)

THE SPIRIT OF THE LAW

SHARE:

Most of us, at some time, wish things were different in our families. If you could create just one law that everyone in your family (including you!) would always keep, what would it be?

EXPLORE:

1 The ten commandments are the laws God gave to his 'family' — the people of God — for all time. Read Exodus 20:1 – 17 and talk about these questions:

▶ **Worshipping God (v 3):** What things or people can become 'gods' in our lives, and why?

▶ **Images of God (v 4 – 6):** What was wrong with making statues of God? Is there any danger in having a mental picture or image of God?

▶ **God's name (v 5):** How might we misuse God's name, as Christians, by the things we do?

▶ **The Sabbath (v 8 – 11):** What is the essence of 'the Sabbath'? How can you ensure that you keep regular sabbaths?

▶ **Parents (v 12):** What does it mean to 'honour' one's parents? Should this command be applied more widely than to one's father and mother?

▶ **Murder (v 13):** What values or people are being destroyed in your community? What steps can you take to revitalise or encourage them?

▶ **Adultery (v 14):** Why does God regard faithfulness in marriage as so important? (See Hosea 3:1; Psalm 100:5; Galatians 5:22.)

▶ **Stealing (v 15):** What things (not just material things) might we steal from others?

▶ **Lying (v 16):** Is lying okay if it doesn't injure others? What about 'white lies'?

▶ **Coveting (v 17):** What antidotes to coveting can you suggest? (See Luke 6:38; 12:29 – 34.)

EXPLORE:

2 How could you restate each command positively, in terms of 'You shall have freedom to...' rather than as 'Thou shalt not...'?

PERSONALLY SPEAKING

One night in a Nigerian dormitory

Comfort Essien will never forget that night in the dormitory in her boarding school in Nigeria which was the turning point in her life.

She was a fifth-former at the time. She had been a regular Bible reader for four years and had become the secretary of the Scripture Union group in her school but found it difficult to recognise that she was a sinner. 'I did not see myself committing some of the obvious sins, but there were times when I knew I fell short of the Bible's standards of Christianity.

'When my parents were praising me for being the best child in the family, somehow within me something would be saying that I was not as good as my parents thought. I knew I told lies, I was stubborn, I used to fight . . . '

But on that decisive night in the dormitory, as Comfort recalls, 'the whole fact of my condition before God became very disturbing to my mind. There was a struggle going on within me. Just before lights-out I reflected on the story of the Prodigal Son and this and other Scriptures became very vivid to me.

'At lights-out I quietly knelt by my bed and faced the fact that I was a sinner, that I was wrong and that I needed God's forgiveness and I invited the Lord Jesus into my heart.

'I must have prayed for over an hour without realising it. It seemed that I was away from the dormitory and in the real presence of God. Peace filled my heart. Before this, when I heard that somebody had died, fear would grip me. I thought, "Supposing you were that person, would you be prepared to face God . . .?"

'I had had a chest pain that the hospital could not diagnose. Doctors told me that I would have to grow up with it. When I had prayed that prayer of repentance in the dormitory, I never told God to heal me because I didn't know a miracle could happen. But that night after sleeping I woke up at twenty to four in the morning and found that the sickness had gone.'

That was nearly twenty years ago. Today Comfort Essien coordinates Scripture Union's schools work in Nigeria.

(Comfort Essien's story is told by Michael Hews in *Outreach* magazine, Autumn 1988.)

PERSONALLY SPEAKING

Held at gunpoint

Lucien Accad, General Secretary of the Bible Society in Lebanon, was driving home from his office in Beirut one evening. When he reached the east-west Beirut checkpoint — a bridge — he and some other travellers were waved over to the side of the road because of a disturbance.

The situation was volatile with the threat that shooting would break out at any moment. But eventually Lucien was allowed to cross the bridge. At the other side he was met by some teenage gunmen, members of 'Hezbullah', who ordered him out of his car.

When they discovered who he was, instead of taking punitive action they aked if he could get them whole Bibles! They had already read one of the Gospels and were keen to know more.

Lucien Accad went on his way, shaking but rejoicing!

(Reported by Tony Dann, Director of Centres' Development, British Youth for Christ.)

59

GOOD NEWS!

Jesus said: 'I have come to give you life — life in all its fullness.'

'GOSPEL' –
WHAT DOES IT MEAN?

A letter drops onto the mat: you've been offered the job! Good news!

You go to the hospital to hear the consultant's report: the growth is not malignant! Good news!

A phone call from your daughter in Australia: she will be able to come back home for Christmas! Good news!

Hope for the future, new life, restored relationships. This is what the gospel is all about. The word 'gospel' is derived from two Anglo-Saxon words, 'god' (good) and 'spel' (words, tidings). It simply means 'good news' and translates the Greek word *euangelion*.

The New Testament concept of good news starts in the Old Testament. The people of Israel went through many national crises; bad news was a part of life. But time and again they experienced the dramatic good news of God breaking in to change the situation, saving them from their enemies (Judges 2:18), bringing forgiveness and peace (Psalm 107:10-16) and establishing justice and righteousness (1 Kings 10:9).

Yet there were still real barriers between God and his people. The changes were only temporary and the people were soon back in their old ways. The Old Testament prophets began to long for a *permanent* inbreaking of God's rule into the lives of his people, and pictured this as a 'new age' heralded by the arrival of a Messiah. God would establish a new covenant with his people under which their very natures would be changed (Jeremiah 31:33-34). 'Your God reigns' (Isaiah 52:7-10) was the good news they longed to hear.

GOOD NEWS ABOUT JESUS

When Jesus started his ministry, he proclaimed that this longed-for reign of God had begun. Good news! Mark tells us exactly what it was that Jesus was saying: ' "The time has come," he said. "The kingdom of God is near. Repent and believe the good news!" ' (Mark 1:14). But the Gospel writers make it clear that Jesus was not simply the *herald* of the good news; he *was* the good news. As Mark writes, it was good news 'about Jesus Christ, the Son of God' (Mark 1:1).

The time has come

In the coming of Jesus many Old Testament prophecies were fulfilled. Matthew in particular draws attention to this in order to prove to his readers that Jesus is the promised Messiah.

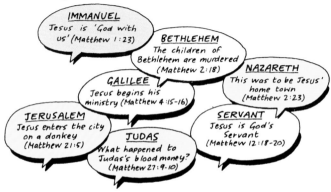

Jesus, too, applied Old Testament prophecies to himself. At the start of his ministry he preached a sermon in the synagogue of his home town, Nazareth, in which he quoted Isaiah 61:1-2 and implied that it spoke of him:

'The Spirit of the Lord is on me,
because he has anointed me
to preach good news to the poor.
He has sent me to proclaim freedom for the prisoners
and recovery of sight for the blind,
to release the oppressed,
to proclaim the year of the Lord's favour.'

Then he told the amazed congregation, 'Today this scripture is fulfilled in your hearing.' (Luke 4:18-21.)

As his life and ministry unfolded, Jesus explained to his disciples how all that was happening was doing so in accordance with what had been prophesied about the Messiah - especially what had been prophesied about his suffering and death (see Mark 8:31; Luke 24:25-27).

As well as being the fulfilment of the prophecies, Jesus saw himself as the fulfilment of the law. 'Do not think,' he said, 'that I have come to abolish the Law or the Prophets; I have not come to abolish them but to fulfil them' (Matthew 5:17).

63

The kingdom of God is near

The arrival of the kingdom, or reign, of God is central to Jesus' proclamation. In the Old Testament, God is portrayed as King over his people, Israel, and as King over all creation. The Jews also looked forward to a future 'Day of the Lord' when God would come in person to reign from Jerusalem over the peoples of the world. During the years between the Testaments the Jews were again subject to oppression by occupying forces – Greece, Syria, Rome – and their hopes for the reign of God took on a political dimension. God would come as a conquering hero, defeating the occupying armies, restoring the land to Israel and establishing her as Number One nation in the world. This was something of a travesty of the hopes of the Old Testament prophets, but by the time of Jesus' coming it had become so popular a view that many were not able to recognise the true arrival of God's kingdom in the person of Jesus.

Jesus' message was:

● **God's world-wide reign had begun with Jesus' arrival:** Jesus showed this by demonstrating God's power over demons, sickness, death and the natural elements. When John the Baptist was in prison awaiting execution, he sent messengers to Jesus to ask him if he really was the Messiah. Jesus' reply pointed him to these things as evidence that God's rule was indeed present in the person of Jesus (Luke 7:18-23).

● **The kingdom of God is the rule of God in human hearts:** It is not a geographical kingdom or political power. Rather, the kingdom is established in the lives of individuals as they give their allegiance to God as king of their lives. God's kingdom is present where people are living in obedience to him, doing his will on earth as it is being done in heaven (Matthew 6:9-13). As such, it has immense social implications. God's rule is one of justice and peace and the subjects of his kingdom will want to work to establish these in the world (Matthew 24:31-46).

November 1989: East German guards begin to demolish the Berlin Wall. The smashing of the wall is a picture of what Jesus came to do – destroying the deadly barrier that held us back from God.

● **The kingdom would become a living reality through Jesus' death and resurrection:** Even Jesus' disciples, right up to the time of his death, thought Jesus would usher in a political kingdom by force and that they would gain privileged positions in it (Mark 10:35-37; Luke 22:24; see also Acts 1:6). Time and again Jesus had to correct them, speaking of his death as the route he had to take to glory, and of himself as 'the way' for them into the kingdom (Mark 8:31-36; John 14:6).

● **The kingdom has still to come in all its fullness:** God's rule has broken into the world in a new way but his activity is still, to some extent, hidden. There will come a day when Jesus returns to the earth and his authority will be established beyond all shadow of doubt. The devil, his angels and evil in all forms will be totally destroyed (Matthew 25:41) and a redeemed society will be formed which will enjoy perfect fellowship with God (Luke 13:29).

Repent and believe

Jesus set up a stark alternative: a person was either in the kingdom of 'this world', and therefore under the power of Satan, or had entered the kingdom of God and was therefore submitting to his rule in his or her life. His call to 'repent' – to turn our backs on the rule of Satan and all that represents in our lives – and to accept the free gift of God's kingdom instead, is urgent and insistent. Like the Old Testament prophets he paints a picture of the future reign of God and the judgment that will bring, and urges people to change their allegiances *now*. This comes out most strongly in his parables: now is the last chance to settle with your opponent before you get flung into prison (Matthew 5:25)! Your deceit has been unearthed, act quickly to avoid the wrath of your employer (Luke 16:1-8)! The bridegroom is coming, hurry to buy oil for your lamps (Matthew 25:1-12) and to put on your wedding garment (Matthew 22:11-13) so that you can join the celebrations!

WHY WERE THE GOSPELS WRITTEN?

At first sight the Gospels appear to be straightforward accounts of the words and deeds of Jesus. But unlike a biography or a history, the Gospels do not provide a consecutive account of Jesus' life. In fact, they tell us almost nothing about him until he was thirty. They set out to provide eye-witness accounts of Jesus' ministry and reflections on its significance, rather than biographical sketches of his whole life. So the material used by the Gospel writers is chosen accordingly: they introduce large blocks of teaching from Jesus' brief, three-year ministry and concentrate on the events surrounding his death.

'People often say... "I'm ready to accept Jesus as a great moral teacher, but I don't accept his claim to be God..." A man who was merely a man and said the sort of things Jesus said would not be a great moral teacher. He would either be a lunatic – on a level with the man who says he is a poached egg – or else he would be the Devil of Hell.'
(C S Lewis, *Mere Christianity*. Glasgow: Collins, 1975)

Before the Gospels were written, their substance would have been passed on orally in the churches as new Christians wanted to find out more about the earthly life of Jesus. As the church spread into places that Jesus had never visited and as the apostles grew old, they realised that their eyewitness accounts of Jesus' ministry had to be preserved for future generations. So the unique 'Gospel' genre was developed. Their accounts were needed for four main purposes:

● **Apologetics:** Those who heard the message and were interested but had questions needed more detailed information about Jesus. Luke wrote, 'Many have undertaken to draw up an account of the things that have been fulfilled among us... since I myself have carefully investigated everything from the beginning, it seemed good also to me to write an orderly account for you, most excellent Theophilus, so that you may know the certainty of the things you have been taught' (Luke 1:1-4).

● **Evangelism:** To challenge the readers with the implications of the message about Jesus: 'These are written that you may believe that Jesus is the Christ, the Son of God, and that by believing you may have life in his name' (John 20:31).

● **Teaching:** New converts in the churches needed information and instruction. While the apostles were there in person they could teach authoritatively: 'They devoted themselves to the apostles' teaching and to the fellowship, to the breaking of bread and to prayer' (Acts 2:42). After their lifetimes their teaching had to be passed on in written form. Mark describes his account in factual terms as 'the gospel about Jesus Christ, the Son of God' (Mark 1:1).

● **Worship:** It is likely that the Gospels were read publicly in the worship meetings of the churches, just as the New Testament letters were.

FOR GROUPS:

FRIENDSHIP EVANGELISM

SHARE:

For many of us evangelism is like guerrilla warfare. We make brief raids into enemy territory then retreat to the safety of our 'holy huddle'. No wonder it seems hard going! In the early church, the gospel often spread from friend to friend or one family member to another. Who first introduced you to Jesus Christ, and how?

READ: John 1:29-51.

EXPLORE:

1 The two disciples follow Jesus because they want to know more about him but they also seem hesitant to question him directly. How can we help our friends feel free to ask us about God?

2 Jesus used a 'come and see' approach with the disciples (v 38-39). Why would this be more effective than just telling them who he was? How can we help our friends to observe Jesus in action?

3 Even in temporary lodgings Jesus seemed to regard hospitality as an important way of allowing others to get to know him (v 39). Why might this approach be important?

4 Note Andrew's hurry and imagine how he tells the news to Simon (v 40-42). If you had been Simon, what would have made you sit up and take notice of what Andrew was saying?

5 Jesus' first six disciples are relatives and acquaintances from a single fishing village (v 44). What advantages and extra challenges are there in trying to introduce to Christ those people with whom we already have close ties — family, neighbours, work colleagues?

6 Jesus is content to let the disciples hang around for months before asking them to make a decision about who he is. Why might it be important not to pressure people into making up their minds about Jesus?

7 Throughout this passage it seems natural for one friend to tell another about Jesus (v 36,41,45). Why do you think we often find this so *unnatural*?

8 What ideas does this passage give you for introducing to Jesus those friends or members of your family who have not yet met him?

(Adapted from Rebecca Pippert and Ruth Siemens, **Evangelism: A Way of Life.** London: Scripture Union, 1986.)

THE WORLD IN WHICH JESUS LIVED

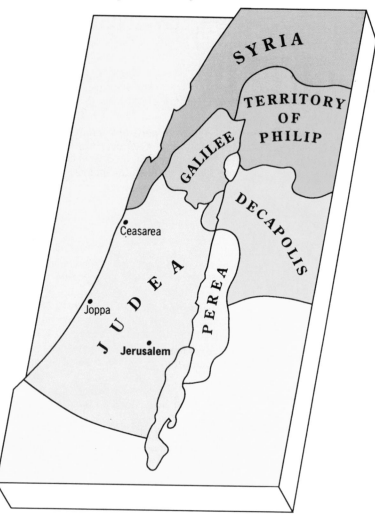

Jesus was a Jew who lived and taught in first-century Palestine; his teaching was directed to actual people in real situations. So it is important to understand the political, cultural and religious climate in which he lived in order to grasp fully the implications of the events and teaching recorded.

The political context

The world into which Jesus was born was politically very volatile. Palestine was under Roman occupation. During Jesus' lifetime Galilee was governed for the most part by the Herods, descendants of Herod Antipater, a half-Jewish adventurer who had been made 'king of the Jews' by Rome. Judea, on the other hand, was ruled mostly by 'procurators' - junior Roman governors who reported to the governors of Syria. Pilate is the best known of these procurators. The Jewish philosopher, Philo, who was a contemporary of Pilate, described him as 'by nature rigid and stubbornly harsh.' Time and again his actions violated Jewish scruples, incensing the people and causing riots and protests.

A strong resistance movement grew up in Palestine and people began to look for a political messiah who would overthrow the Romans. But insurrections were ruthlessly put down.

There were many tensions and divisions among the Jewish people at that time. The Zealots were a party of extreme nationalists who resisted payment of taxes to Rome; it is possible that 'Simon the Zealot', one of Jesus' disciples, belonged to this group. At the other extreme were those who decided to make the most of a bad situation and so became tax collectors for the Romans. They were despised and hated as collaborators by their fellow Jews. Jesus' disciple, Matthew, came from their ranks.

There was also intrigue and constant political manoeuvering among the Roman governors and procurators. Pilate's fear of stepping out of line comes through clearly in the account of Jesus' trial.

The cultural context

● **The dispersion of Jews from Palestine:** By the time of Jesus Jews were scattered throughout the eastern Mediterranean area. Some had been forcibly deported in the exiles from Samaria and Jerusalem in 722, 597 and 587 BC. Others had migrated to centres of growing importance, such as Alexandria. By the time of Christ between one half and two thirds of all Jews were living outside Palestine.

Those Jews still living in Palestine held mixed attitudes towards Jews of the dispersion. Those who had strongly maintained their Jewish faith were largely accepted. They paid their annual temple tax and would make pilgrimages to the temple in Jerusalem for the major festivals. Those who had decided to intermarry with the people among whom they were living, and had buried their Jewish identity, were generally despised. The Samaritans feature in the Gospels as a people despised for being neither fully Jew nor fully Gentile. They regarded themselves as descendants of those Israelites who had been exiled after the fall of Samaria but most Jews would have nothing to do with them. Against this background it becomes clear that Jesus' dealings with Samaritans were unconventional and significant.

● **Greek language and culture:** After the death of Alexander the Great, who had conquered the entire eastern Mediterranean between 336 and 323 BC, Palestine was ruled by the Ptolemies, a succession of Hellenistic kings. They were happy to let the Jews govern themselves as far as religion went and, under their benevolent rule, Greek language and culture came to dominate the commercial and educational life of Palestine. The Hebrew scriptures were translated into Greek and the common Greek dialect, *Koine* Greek, became an international language. This was the language in which the New Testament was written though Aramaic remained the common language of the Jews in Palestine. The widespread use of *Koine* Greek, combined with the network of roads built and maintained by the Romans, enabled the gospel message to spread quickly to the surrounding countries.

The first Christians lived in a world heavily influenced by Greek culture. The Greeks were highly sophisticated. This bath-house in Ephesus even boasted under-floor heating!

The religious context

In 280 BC the Ptolemies lost their grip on Palestine and the land fell into the control of the Seleucids. Antiochus Epiphanes, a fanatical Hellenist, came to the throne in 175 BC and determined to make Palestine a loyal Seleucid province by imposing Hellenistic culture and religion on its inhabitants. He ordered Jews to 'abandon their ancestral customs and live no longer by the laws of God,' and this naturally provoked extreme opposition. The main religious groupings we read about in the Gospels originated during this period or shortly after.

● **Pharisees:** These were an offshoot of the *Hasidim*, the 'faithful' or 'devoted' ones, mostly from the poorer strata of society, who had stood out against the innovations of Antiochus Epiphanes. The Pharisees were concerned that God's law should be kept strictly. They were a group which began with high motives and had a strong following among the common people but they tended towards legalism, keeping the letter of the law but disregarding its spirit. It is for this hypocrisy that they come in for sharp rebuke from Jesus.

● **Sadducees:** These were men associated with the priestly families. They were either priests themselves ('Sadducee' probably derives from 'Zadok', the high priest of David's day from whom the high priests were descended) or were related to them in some way. They were generally wealthy and politically influential, and were often willing to compromise with the pagan rulers of Palestine. They figure most prominently in the Gospels because of their insistence that there is no resurrection from the dead.

● **Scribes:** These were the interpreters and teachers of the Mosaic law, having taken over this role from the priests and Levites after the exile. In the Gospels they are often linked with the Pharisees as they agreed with their stress on the importance of the law. Many of them probably were Pharisees. They were strongly opposed to Jesus because he refused to adhere to the 'oral tradition' – all the man-made laws surrounding and interpreting the Torah – which they taught.

THE STYLE OF JESUS' TEACHING

It is clear from the Gospels that Jesus was an outstanding teacher. Crowds of thousands flocked to hear him speak and would stay listening to him for hours, apparently forgetting even about the need to eat (Matthew 14:13-21)! The authority with which he taught was compelling (Matthew 7:28-29): the people recognised him to be a prophet. But his style must have been highly memorable too, as the teaching that has come down to us in the Gospels is succinct, imaginative and poetic – designed to be learnt and passed on to others.

Jesus used a number of verbal devices in his teaching and it is important to recognise these if his words are not to be misunderstood.

Parable

The Greek term *parabole* is used in the Gospels of a wide variety of figures of speech, such as proverbs, riddles and metaphors.

All Jesus' parables were means of telling his listeners something about the kingdom of God – its nature, its coming, values, growth and the sacrifices for which it calls. Their object was to jolt people into seeing, perhaps for the first time, what the kingdom was really all about. Supremely, the parables were about Jesus himself, giving the hearers insight into who he was. People's failure to understand who Jesus was resulted in their failure to understand his parables.

Generally, when reading the 'story' parables, we should look for the main point that Jesus was making. Some of Jesus' parables were, however, 'clearly intended to illustrate *several* lessons, as in the parable of the prodigal son, where stress is laid on the joy which God as Father has in forgiving his children, the nature of repentance, and the sin of jealousy and self-righteousness.' (I.H. Marshall, 'Parable' in *The Illustrated Bible Dictionary*. Leicester: IVP, 1980.)

Steps to understanding the parables

1 Look for the one main point Jesus is making.

2 Look to see what the original context was in which Jesus spoke the parable. (Who was there? What had just been said or done? How had people reacted?)

3 Look to see how the Gospel-writer interpreted the parable. (What teaching or incident does he put before it? What comes after it? Does he give an explanation for the parable?)

4 Ask yourself, 'What is God saying to me today through this parable?' (How are my attitudes the same as those of the people in the parable? How are they different? What similar action do I need to take? Are there priorities I need to rethink?)

There are a number of reasons why Jesus taught in parables:

● **To call people to action:** All the story-parables of Jesus call for a response. The hearer has to *do* something – and quickly! – to get ready for the King whose rule has already begun.

● **To disarm his listeners:** Jesus sometimes pre-empted a verbal attack from his opponents, or showed up their faults, by telling a story. When he got to the punch line his opponents realised Jesus had answered their objections even before they raised them. Those who were self-righteously writing off others as being too common or bad for God to care about were suddenly faced with the truth that the opposite was actually the case.

The story told to Simon the Pharisee (Luke 7:36-50) combines both these elements, as well as giving radically different messages to Simon and to the woman whose action triggered the conversation.

'Now one of the Pharisees invited Jesus to have dinner with him, so he went to the Pharisee's house and reclined at the table. When a woman who had lived a sinful life in that town learned that Jesus was eating at the Pharisee's house, she brought an alabaster jar of perfume, and as she stood behind him at his feet weeping, she began to wet his feet with her tears. Then she wiped them with her hair, kissed them and poured perfume on them.

When the Pharisee who had invited him saw this, he said to himself, "If this man were a prophet, he would know who is touching him and what kind of woman she is – that she is a sinner."

Jesus answered him, "Simon, I have something to tell you."

"Tell me, teacher," he said.

"Two men owed money to a certain money-lender. One owed him five hundred denarii, and the other fifty. Neither of them had the money to pay him back, so he cancelled the debts of both. Now which of them will love him more?"

Simon replied, "I suppose the one who had the bigger debt cancelled."

"You have judged correctly," Jesus said.

Then he turned towards the woman and said to Simon, "Do you see this woman? I came into your house. You did not give me any water for my feet, but she wet my feet with her tears and wiped them with her hair... I tell you, her many sins have been forgiven – for she loved much. But he who has been forgiven little loves little..."

Jesus said to the woman, "Your faith has saved you; go in peace." '

Simon would have heard a strong call to repentance in this story. What the woman would have heard, however, was that God fully accepted her.

Other examples of parables intended to disarm Jesus' audience are: the parable of the good Samaritan (Luke 10:25-37); the parable of the lost son (Luke 15:1-2, 11- 32) and the parable of the tenants (Mark 11:27-12:12).

● **To illustrate his message:** Then, as now, a vivid image stuck in people's minds longer than a careful, wordy explanation. The parable of the rich fool (Luke 16:1-8) is a graphic illustration of a wealthy man so bound up with making money that he doesn't stop to think why he's spending his life that way – until it's too late. Although Jesus had said, 'Love your neighbour as yourself' (Mark 12:31), the picture of the despised Samaritan binding up the wounds of the mugged Jew, hit home in a way the words could not (Luke 10:25-37).

● **To conceal his teaching from his opponents:** Opponents of Jesus were always dogging him. Jealous of his influence and fearful for their own position, they looked for ways to discredit him in the eyes of the people. When Jesus turned over the tables of the money changers in the temple, he publicly challenged the civil and religious authority of the Saducees. By pointing out the hypocrisy of the Pharisees Jesus threatened their self-righteous security, as well as their religious leadership. So they tried hard to make Jesus 'open his mouth and put his foot in it' so that they would have grounds for accusing him before the Romans of disloyalty and insurrection. A straight message about the kingdom of God from someone thought to be the 'Messiah' or 'Christ' could easily be misrepresented as a challenge to the supremacy of the Roman empire. But the Pharisees and Saducees would have to work very hard to make the Romans believe that stories about grains of mustard seed or yeast in bread dough posed a serious threat to the stability of the empire.

● **To prevent those 'outside' the kingdom from understanding his message:** There may be another reason for Jesus' speaking in parables. In Mark 4:11-12 Jesus quoted Isaiah and seemed to imply that he spoke in parables so that 'those on the outside' would *not* understand. Scholars still debate how this should be interpreted. Was Jesus deliberately obscuring the truth from some people? After all he also said, 'No one knows the Son except the Father, and no one knows the Father except the Son and those to whom the Son chooses to reveal him' (Matthew 11:27). Most commentators, however, believe that Jesus' statement is to be taken as a statement of fact, rather than a statement of intent. That is, even though he taught the people carefully and vividly about the kingdom of God, there were some who deliberately turned away from him, closing their ears to what he had to say.

PERSONALLY SPEAKING

Bible under the blankets

There were seven kids plus Gran living in our three-bedroomed house, so it was a relief for Mum to get rid of the younger ones to Sunday school on Sunday morning (and afternoon!).

We were a happy pagan family and my brothers and sisters had all drifted away from Sunday school by the time they reached their teens — but I didn't. I was a keen reader and very early on the Scripture Union lady in my church (all I can remember about her is that she was old!) gave me Scripture Union notes to help me read the King James version which my Grandma had given to me.

I can clearly remember night after night reading my Bible with the notes by torch light in my top bunk bed. It became one of those routine patterns which so delight us in childhood.

I don't remember becoming a Christian but, through the Bible and my church, I simply grew up with Jesus. I didn't know anything then about the complexities of interpretation which I now have to teach students but, day by day, I grew to understand the Word and learnt how to apply it to my daily living. The short prayers in the Scripture Union notes taught me how to pray simply and practically. And now, by the grace of God, I'm able to spend my days helping others.

Nick Mercer
(Nick Mercer is the Director of Training at London Bible College.)

Symbolic actions

On a number of occasions Jesus taught by something he did, rather than by what he said. His action was often carefully planned so that it would be instructive for the audience he had in mind. Although the action spoke for itself, Jesus would sometimes follow it with an explanation:

'The evening meal was being served... (Jesus) got up from the meal, took off his outer clothing, and wrapped a towel round his waist. After that, he poured water into a basin and began to wash his disciples' feet, drying them with the towel that was wrapped around him...

When he had finished washing their feet, he put on his clothes and returned to his place. "Do you understand what I have done for you?" he asked them... "Now that I, your Lord and Teacher, have washed your feet, you also should wash one another's feet." '(John 13:2-14)

Other examples of Jesus' symbolic action or 'acted parables' are:

► **His calling Zacchaeus down from the tree:** indicating that the kingdom of God is offered to all people (Luke 19:1-10).

► **The triumphal entry:** Jesus claims to be the messianic figure of Zechariah 9:9 (Mark 11:1-11).

► **The fig tree withers at Jesus' command:** Jesus warns of inevitable imminent judgment (Mark 11:12-14, 20-21).

► **Jesus overturns the tables of the money changers in the temple:** another warning of judgment (Mark 11:15-18).

► **Jesus selects twelve disciples:** he is establishing a 'new Israel' which is both a continuation of the old one yet also the beginning of a new people of God (Mark 3:13-19).

Poetry

Jesus' sayings in the Gospels are often written in the form of poetry. Usually they are not translated as poetry so it is not easy to recognise. In its original form this poetry didn't rhyme but had rythmic balance, rather like the psalms:

'If a kingdom is divided against itself,
    that kingdom cannot stand.
If a house is divided against itself,
    that house cannot stand.'
                        (Mark 3:24-25)

'Ask and it will be given to you;
    seek and you will find;
    knock, and the door will be opened to you.
For everyone who asks receives;
    He who seeks finds;
    and to him who knocks, the door will be opened.'
                        (Matthew 7:7-8)

'Whoever exalts himself
    will be humbled,
and whoever humbles himself
    will be exalted.'
                        (Matthew 23:12)

Overstatement

Overstating your case to make a point forcibly was a feature of Semitic speech.

For example, Jesus could have said:

> Your loyalty to me should be so great that even the strong bonds of love and loyalty to close relatives pale into insignificance beside it.

Instead, he put the challenge much more powerfully:

> If anyone comes to me and does not hate his father and mother, his wife and children, his brothers and sisters — yes, even his own life — he cannot be my disciple!
>
> Luke 14:26

Similarly, he could have said:

> No sin is so pleasant that it is worth going to hell over. Tear out of your life anything that keeps you away from God.

But what he actually said is much more graphic:

> If your right eye causes you to sin, gouge it out and throw it away. It is better for you to lose one part of your body than for your whole body to be thrown into hell.
>
> Matthew 5:29-30

Such overstatements should not be taken literally!

WHY FOUR DIFFERENT GOSPELS?

The fact that we have four Gospels in the New Testament is no accident. The different accounts were written to meet the needs of a variety of communities of believers. Mark's Gospel was probably the first to be written and was then 'rewritten' twice by Matthew and Luke to meet the very different needs of other communities. Most scholars think that John's Gospel was written independently of the other three, to meet yet another need.

There is no warrant, however, for setting the four Gospels in opposition to each other, as though their interpretations of the events they narrate are mutually incompatible. They stand alongside each other in the New Testament canon as equally authoritative accounts of the life, death and ministry of Jesus. Far from detracting from their truthfulness this fourfold approach is their strength. As Howard Marshall writes, 'The greatness of this person could not have been captured in one picture. So we have four portraits, each bringing out its own distinctive facets of the character of Jesus.' (I H Marshall, quoted in (eds) D and P Alexander, **Handbook to the Bible.** Tring: Lion Publishing, 1973.)

The first three Gospels are often referred to as the 'synoptic' ('same view') Gospels because they see the ministry of Jesus from broadly the same point of view. Each follows the same general outline tracing the early life of Jesus, his baptism and temptations; the course of his ministry in Galilee, Samaria and Judea; the passion week and Jesus' death and resurrection. John's Gospel is significantly different from these in style and approach.

To understand the full gospel message we need to take seriously the way it is presented and interpreted by each of these four writers. What were their main emphases and for whom might they have been writing?

Matthew, Mark, Luke – authors of the 'Synoptic Gospels' which share much material in common.

John – author of the fourth Gospel, which was written independently of the other three.

The message of Matthew

Matthew was writing primarily for Jewish Christians and was seeking to prove to them that Jesus is their Messiah. Yet he did not ignore Gentile readers; his Gospel may well have answered their questions about the Jewish origins of the Christian faith. The main points of his message are these:

● **The Messiah:** Jesus is the long-awaited Messiah. He perfectly fulfils all the Old Testament prophecies.

● **Christian lifestyle:** With pastoral concern, Matthew emphasises the spiritual and ethical nature of living in the kingdom.

● **The church:** It is only Matthew who records Jesus' teaching about the church: its basis (16:16-18); its authority to discipline its members (18:18); its life of prayer and worship (18:20); its work of teaching, discipling and baptising (28:19-20).

● **A missionary concern:** While Matthew writes for a Jewish Christian readership he emphasises that the kingdom of heaven is open to people of every nation.

Mark probably wrote his Gospel in Rome. Christians there were already suffering the first waves of Roman persecution. The Coliseum is a symbol of the sufferings endured by many Christians within its walls.

The message of Mark

Mark probably wrote his Gospel for Gentile readers, possibly those living in Rome. His purpose was evangelistic, wanting to tell them the facts that prove Jesus was the Son of God (1:1). He emphasises:

● **The humanity of Jesus:** Mark portrays him as fully human, feeling compassion, anger, sorrow, tenderness and love.

● **The divinity of Jesus:** Mark emphasises his power over evil spirits, illnesses and nature. At Jesus' death a Roman centurion exclaims, 'Surely this man was the Son of God!'

● **The redemptive work of Jesus:** The narrative of Mark's Gospel moves swiftly and compellingly towards the events of the passion. He records Jesus' saying that he had come 'to give his life as a ransom for many' (10:45). This emphasis is in full accord with early Christian preaching, which centred on the cross of Christ (eg 1 Corinthians 15:3-8; Philippians 2:5-11; 1 Peter 2:21-24).

The message of Luke

Luke starts his Gospel by stating its purpose. He wrote it for Theophilus, presumably a high-ranking, wealthy Roman, who had already received some instruction in the Christian faith. At the same time he writes for all other Gentiles with a similar interest to discover the historical origin of Christianity. Luke's record of the beginning and development of Christianity is in two parts, Luke and Acts. The main features of his message are:

● **Jesus is the Saviour of Gentiles:** Luke is concerned to show that Jesus did not die only for Jews but for Gentiles too.

● **Jesus' concern for the disadvantaged:** As a doctor, Luke seems to have had a particular interest in people and noted Jesus' own concern for the materially poor, social outcasts, women and children. Luke shares Jesus' respect for and acceptance of these groups of people. In particular, he devotes much space to the significant part played by women in the events of Jesus' early life, ministry, death and resurrection.

● **The gospel of Christ is not subversive:** It is likely that Theophilus was concerned about the potentially subversive nature of Jesus' teaching. It seems that Luke wanted to counter any ill-founded, derogatory reports about Jesus that Theophilus might have heard. It is possible that Luke's continuing account in Acts has a similar purpose, explaining the nature of the church and the way in which Christianity spread.

● **The themes of prayer, the Holy Spirit and joy:** Luke tells Theophilus about the importance of prayer, the power of the Holy Spirit and the joy that comes in accepting the good news of the gospel. Luke records the significance of each of these in the life of Jesus, as well as in the lives of the disciples.

The message of John

John's Gospel is strikingly different from the other three. It is primarily theological, plunging straight in with an affirmation of the pre-existence, deity and humanity of Christ. Like Luke, however, John tells us why he has written his Gospel: 'that you may believe that Jesus is the Christ, the Son of God, and that by believing you may have life in his name' (20:31). The Gospel is like an evangelistic tract. The reader is given an account of only seven of Jesus' miracles, but these are generally followed by teaching explaining the inner meaning of what Jesus was doing. The two main elements of John's message are:

● **The evidence:** A number of witnesses are brought to the attention of the reader, in order to show that Jesus is the Christ, the Son of God: the Old Testament, John the Baptist, people in general who lived alongside him, the apostles, God the Father, the Holy Spirit, Jesus' works, Jesus himself in his words and claims. Like a jury, the reader is expected to make up his or her mind about who Jesus is on the strength of these witnesses.

● **The verdict:** As John brings forward the witnesses he also records the verdicts that were reached by various groups who encountered Jesus. Some people rejected him. Others responded to him, listening to him, believing in him, learning the truth about him, loving him and one another. These latter verdicts present to John's readers both a model of belief and the challenge to believe.

THE PARABLE OF THE VINEYARD WORKERS

SHARE:

What would/do you expect from a good employer?

READ: Matthew 20:1-6

EXPLORE:

1 Imagine that you had 'borne the burden of the work and the heat of the day' (20:12) yet were paid the same as those who worked only an hour. How would you feel and why? What factors do you think should determine a person's wages or salary?

2 This parable springs from discussion about an earlier incident. Read about this in Matthew 19:16-22. If someone had asked the rich young man how to gain eternal life, what do you think he would have said (see especially v 16)?

3 Does Jesus' answer (v 17) to this question surprise you? Why or why not? What do you think he was trying to point out to the young man (vs 19,21)?

4 Why is it not possible for *anyone* to enter the kingdom of God (gain eternal life) by keeping the commandments (see Romans 3:9-12, 23)?

5 Why do you think Jesus told this parable after the incident with the young man?

6 What makes God (represented by the vineyard owner) *unlike* an employer (see Romans 6:23)?

7 What is the good news this parable gives about the way we may gain eternal life?

8 Even when we are Christians, we can still think of God as our 'employer'. How far do you think of God like this? How does this affect the way you feel about the 'work' you do for him?

9 In the Bible, God's relationship to us is never pictured in terms of employer and employee. What pictures might you suggest instead to describe the relationship that God wants between himself and us? Explain your suggestions. You may like to compare the story Jesus told in Luke 15:11-32, especially verses 25-27.

10 How does this passage help you to see your service to God in proper perspective?

PERSONALLY SPEAKING

In Thailand, costly discipleship

Yawanit Kasaetwatananond was the first member of her family to become a Christian. When she first professed her faith at school at the age of fourteen, it was a very costly thing to do in a strongly Buddhist country.

It was costly at home too. On special worship days she couldn't join in the family meal because the food had first been offered to idols. So she used to save up money and eat out on those days. Since then four of her brothers and sisters have become Christians.

Yawanit was approached by Scripture Union and was asked to join their staff, but at that time she also had three other options: to take up the offer of a scholarship to study in Australia; to accept a proposal of marriage from her boyfriend; or to continue in her teaching post in the far north of Thailand.

She agreed to pray about the invitation from Scripture Union for one month. One morning during that time she came to John 12:12-26 in her Scripture Union daily readings.

That morning, as she recalls, 'I was challenged by the Lord, "If you are a grain of wheat, have you ever dropped yourself into the earth?"

'I had two other problems about Scripture Union's invitation. I didn't feel I was capable, but I read that morning that the Lord will be with whoever serves him. Also, to be a qualified teacher in Thailand is quite something and it was hard to leave a teaching post to become Miss Nobody, but I read that morning that "Whoever serves me, I'll honour you" and God's honour is everlasting.

'Although the way ahead had looked dark and uncertain at the time, I promptly wrote accepting the invitation.'

That was in 1975. Since then, under Yawanit's leadership, God has enabled the Scripture Union movement in Thailand to grow. In 1987 they were able to begin schools work in Christian schools attended by many children from non-Christian backgrounds.

(Yawanit Kasaetwatananond is the General Secretary of Scripture Union in Thailand. Her story is told by Michael Hews in *Outreach* magazine, Autumn 1988.)

PERSONALLY SPEAKING

At school in Sierra Leone

Amos Lavaly was a second-year student at a secondary school at Bo in Sierra Leone when an American woman missionary gave him some Bible reading notes. He recalls:

'I felt that daily Bible reading would disturb my school work . . . so I decided to read the Bible until the end of the holidays and then stop. But strange things started happening to me – I was feeling very unhappy and uncomfortable.

'I had a burning urge to read my Bible . . . I finally decided to fix a definite time for daily reading, immediately after school in the afternoon. As I continued reading my Bible day after day I realised for the first time in my life that I was a sinner. God spoke to me through his book, the Bible. I then asked God to forgive my sins and I yielded my life completely to him.'

Amos began to pray for other boys in the school. By the time he left, sixty were meeting together regularly to read the Bible and pray.

(Amos Lavaly is now a University lecturer and is on the National Committee of Scripture Union in Sierra Leone. His story is recorded in *This Faith Works*. Africa Christian Press.)

ARE THE GOSPELS HISTORICALLY RELIABLE?

Many people think that because the Gospels were produced two thousand years ago they must be full of errors and discrepancies. However, when examined on the same terms as other historical documents the grounds for accepting their reliability are very compelling.

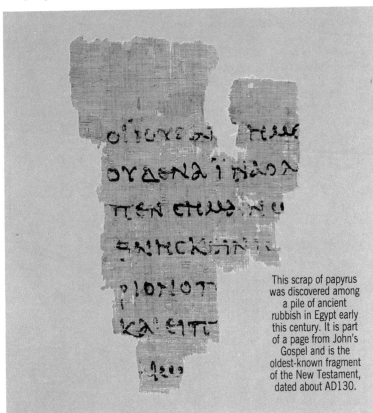

This scrap of papyrus was discovered among a pile of ancient rubbish in Egypt early this century. It is part of a page from John's Gospel and is the oldest-known fragment of the New Testament, dated about AD130.

The accuracy of the manuscripts

The accuracy of the original autographs can be gauged from the number and corresponding accuracy of copies of them and from the time gap between the writing of the original documents and the earliest existing copies of them. The shorter this time gap the more accurate the copies are likely to be. The more copies there are the better one can be compared with another to deduce the likely wording of the original autographs. On these two counts the New Testament documents would appear to be far more reliable than many other documents of a similar period whose accuracy is generally accepted without question. Professor F F Bruce highlights the difference between the New Testament manuscripts and other ancient historical works:

● 'For Caesar's *Gallic War* (composed between 58 and 50 BC) there are several extant manuscripts, but only nine or ten are good and the oldest is some 900 years later than Caesar's day.'

● 'Of the 142 books of the Roman History of Livy (59 BC − AD 17) only thirty-five survive; these are known to us from not more than twenty manuscripts of any consequence, only one of which... is as old as the fourth century.'

● 'Of the fourteen books of the *Histories* of Tacitus (c AD 100) only four and a half survive; of the sixteen books of his *Annals*, ten survive in full and two in part. The text of these extant portions of his two great historical works depends entirely on two manuscripts, one of the ninth century and one of the eleventh.'

In contrast with these, 'There are in existence about 5000 Greek manuscripts of the new Testament in whole or in part. The best and most important of these go back to somewhere about AD 350.' In addition, 'considerable fragments remain of papyrus copies of books of the New Testament dated from 100 to 200 years earlier still.' A fragment of John's Gospel, dated around AD 130, only forty years or so after its first composition, has also been discovered.

(F F Bruce, **The New Testament Documents: Are they reliable?** Leicester: IVP, 1960)

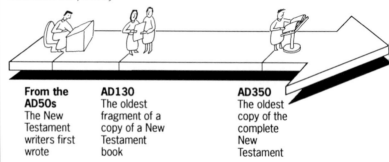

From the AD50s
The New Testament writers first wrote

AD130
The oldest fragment of a copy of a New Testament book

AD350
The oldest copy of the complete New Testament

The accuracy of the oral tradition

Before the Gospels were written down various elements in their content, such as the teaching of Jesus, would have been passed on by word of mouth. If this had happened in modern western society it is very likely that the teaching would have been embellished or distorted as it was related. It is most unlikely that this would have been the case in a first-century Palestinian setting. This is for two reasons:

● **The tradition of oral learning:** All Jewish boys were trained to learn by heart vast tracts of the Old Testament scriptures. The accurate relaying of stories and reminiscences about Jesus would have posed no problem to them.

● **The style of Jesus' teaching:** The rabbis took great pains to ensure that their sayings were passed on accurately by word of mouth among their followers. They devised their teaching in such a way that it would be memorable. It has been suggested that Jesus taught his disciples in the same way, formulating his teaching into pithy, proverbial sayings and stories that would make it easy to remember.

AREN'T THEY BIASED?

This question is closely related to the first one. The texts might be reliable but how do we know the accounts they contain are utterly honest? After all, the early church had a vested interest in portraying Jesus as the Son of God, the Messiah.

Many people are sceptical about the miracles and the resurrection of Jesus. And yet this was probably true of the people who lived in the time of Jesus, saw the miracles for themselves and later wrote about them!

It is obvious and undeniable that the Gospel writers believed that Jesus was the Son of God, the redeemer of the world. They were, indeed, prepared to die for this belief. But this does not automatically mean that they wrote accounts of him that were less than truthful. On the contrary, it would be surprising if they bore witness to the one who claimed to be *the* truth by anything other than truthful accounts of his life and ministry. It is similarly unlikely that they would be prepared to die for beliefs they knew to be doubtful.

A number of features indicate the complete honesty and reliability of the Gospel writers.

● **Honesty about the apostles:** If the early church had been concerned more with giving itself a good press than with presenting the truth, it would have ensured that the apostles – the early church leaders – were presented in a much better light than they are. Just as the Old Testament historians painted Israel's 'great' figures 'warts and all', so the Gospel writers present the disciples in their true colours. They are shown afraid, squabbling, failing to understand Jesus' teaching, proud, weak, even denying and deserting Christ. This hardly compares with the sort of biographical material the Tory party might select if it wanted to commend members of the cabinet to the general public!

● **Honesty would not necessarily work to their advantage:** For example, John's Gospel is sometimes accused of being anti-semitic as it is generally very critical of 'the Jews'. For a considerable part of the first century Christianity was a 'protected' religion in the Roman Empire, being seen as merely a branch of Judaism. Writings such as John's would have tended to make the differences, and even antagonisms, clearer and reduced the chances of Christianity's legal protection.

● **The facts could be checked:** The Gospels were written only about forty years after the death of Jesus. There were still many people around who could verify the truth or otherwise of their reports and these people were not always sympathetic to followers of 'the Way'. As F F Bruce points out: 'It was not friendly eyewitnesses that the early preachers had to reckon with; there were others less well disposed who were also conversant with the main facts of the ministry and death of Jesus. The disciples could not afford to risk inaccuracies (not to speak of wilful manipulation of the facts), which would at once be exposed by those who would be only too glad to do so.' (F F Bruce, **The New Testament Documents: Are they reliable?** Leicester: IVP, 1960.)

WHAT ABOUT THE MIRACLES?

As we have seen, miracles were integral to the message of Jesus: the reign of God had begun with his coming; the effects of the overthrow of Satan were visible. Demons were being cast out, the sick were healed, natural elements and processes were being over-ridden by the Lord of nature.

Because the miracles make important theological statements about Jesus, their historicity is sometimes doubted. The views of Rudolf Bultmann, a New Testament scholar born in Germany in 1884, have been highly influential among many modern theologians. He believed that the world-view pre-supposed by the New Testament writers has been outgrown by modern man. Whereas first-century people believed in a supernatural world and in a personal God who intervened in the lives of ordinary people, twentieth-century people could not.

'It is impossible to use electric light and the wireless and to avail ourselves of modern medical and surgical discoveries and at the same time to believe in the New Testament world of spirits and miracles.' (R Bultmann, **New Testament and Mythology**, in Hans Werner Bartsch (ed), **Kerygma and Myth** vol 1. London: SPCK, 1964.)

Bultmann's solution was to reinterpret the teaching of the Gospels in a way that, he believed, got across their basic message in a form that twentieth-century people could accept. At heart, this is a message about man and his ability to live an 'authentic' life, rather than about God and man's relationship to him. Bultmann spoke of faith, for instance, as the ability 'to open ourselves freely to the future'.

However, in attempting to reinterpret in this way the Gospels' accounts of such things as the miracles of Jesus and the resurrection, Bultmann denied any historical, objective basis for the Christian faith. The apostle Paul, however, insisted that the historical truth of the events of Jesus' life, death and resurrection are vital if the gospel is going to say anything worth hearing (1 Corinthians 15:14).

Jesus' miracles 'were signs of his mission to those who were willing to believe in him. They were never intended as proofs to force mental acceptance on those unwilling to set up a relationship of faith and obedience with him.'
*(Roger Forster and Paul Marston, **That's a good question.** Eastbourne: Kingsway, 1977.)*

There are several factors to take into account when considering whether the miracles recorded in the Gospels should be taken literally.

● **Theological truth depends on historical truth:** It is not necessary to conclude that because the miracles of Jesus illustrate theological truth the accounts of them are purely fictitious. On the contrary, New Testament Christianity claimed to be solidly founded on fact (1 Corinthians 15:3-7,14-20; 1 John 1:1-3), as did the Judaism from which it grew.

● **First-century people were not especially gullible:** It has been suggested that the common people who followed the outstanding rabbi called Jesus were so enamoured with him that they ascribed miraculous powers to him. Yet there are no grounds for supposing that they were any more gullible than twentieth-century westerners. Some, in fact, took a lot of convincing; Jesus' actions were just as challenging to their presuppositions about the 'laws of nature' as they are to ours (see John 9:1-41).

● **The records are part of the 'scientific evidence':** Miracles are often discounted on the grounds that they are 'unscientific'. Yet the New Testament records are highly regarded for their accuracy and must be taken into account as part of the scientific evidence that miracles do happen. A scientist may not discount evidence just because it scuppers his theory.

● **The resurrection:** This, the most stunning event recorded in the Gospels, has never been disproved. The dead body of Jesus was never found, whereas the living, risen Jesus appeared to as many as five hundred people at one time (1 Corinthians 15:6). Only if this can be disproved can the other miracles recorded in the Gospels be discounted.

● **Jesus was God:** If Jesus really was who he claimed to be there is no problem in accepting the miracles as true accounts of his actions. The onus is on those who do not accept the miracles to prove that Jesus was not the Son of God.

WHAT ABOUT THE CONTRADICTIONS?

The four Gospels sometimes appear to contradict each other, giving conflicting information or setting incidents in the life of Jesus at different times in his ministry. But the conflicts are more apparent than real.

John's Gospel describes a healing Jesus worked at the Pool of Bethesda in Jerusalem, which had 'five porches'. In 1914 the pool was discovered 30 feet below street level, disproving those who claimed that the pool had been 'invented' by John.

● **Four perspectives:** Like present-day newspaper journalists, the Gospel writers were writing from different perspectives, with different reasons and for different 'audiences'. Matthew, with his eye for church teaching programmes, tended to group Jesus' teachings topically, rather than chronologically. For example, in chapter 13, he gathers together eight of Jesus' parables about the kingdom of heaven.

● **The possibility of harmonising:** It is usually possible to harmonise apparently conflicting accounts. For example, John places the cleansing of the temple at the start of Jesus' ministry (John 2:12-17); Luke places it at the end (Luke 19:45-46). There is no reason, however, why there should not have been two such incidents.

● **The discoveries of archaeology:** Until recently, John in particular was thought to have invented much of the detail of his accounts because his Gospel seemed so obviously to be 'theological' rather than historical. It was supposed, for instance, that his account of the healing of a crippled man at the pool of Bethesda (John 5:1-8) must have been fictitious, as the pool had never been found, nor were there any other records of such a pool ever having existed. But archaelogical excavations in 1914 did bring the pool to light, matching exactly John's description of it. Time and again in this way the Gospel writers have proved themselves to be painstaking researchers and accurate writers.

PERSONALLY SPEAKING

Follow Me!

'Follow ME and I will make you fishers of men', Mark 1:17. Like a sharp arrow well aimed, these words leapt out from the pages of my text-book and pierced my heart.

It was an ordinary lecture in Religious Education in an ordinary school. I had no particular interest in the Christ or the Jesus person. However 'The Life of Christ' was listed as one of the options in the Arts stream and I was determined to obtain my matriculation, so I had decided to study it out of academic interest. I was attending Wray's High School in Croal Street, Georgetown, in British Guiana as it was then. The teacher asked me to read verses 14-19 of the first chapter of Mark's Gospel. As I read, I became aware of a strange Presence and the whole atmosphere changed. The classroom became a holy place. It was as

though JESUS stood there gazing down at me. Something different was happening to me. His eyes, gentle loving eyes which went right through me, left me feeling exposed and naked. It was as though time stopped. The moments seemed to hang in the air in one eternal suspense. There was a sweet warm strength and beauty emanating from this person. As He lifted his hand and pointed his finger in a beckoning manner, I could hear a soft yet authoritative voice deep inside me saying 'FOLLOW ME . . .' It was gentle yet irresistible. I was arrested . . .

My ambitions to become a medical doctor and surgeon, my dreams of becoming a practising Hindu priest, my desire to fight for the political and economic freedom of our people were now challenged by the claims of Christ upon my life.'

(Philip Mohabir, *Building Bridges.* London: Hodder and Stoughton. 1988)

The prophets spoke and acted with the authority and power of God.

WHO WERE THE PROPHETS?

The biblical books generally regarded as 'prophetic' are those which fall between (and include) Isaiah and Malachi in the Old Testament. But prophecy is not limited to these books and the prophets whose oracles they record. This is because 'prophecy' in the Bible is as much a matter of *forthtelling* - speaking out God's message for his people - as it is of *foretelling* - predicting the future. So we find prophecy in the history books of the Old and New

Prophet	Approximate dates of ministry (BC)	King(s)	Kingdom
THE EARLY, 'NON-WRITING' PROPHETS			
Samuel	1050 – 1000	Saul, David	United
Elijah	870 – 852	Ahab, Ahaziah	Israel
Elisha	852 – 795	Jehoram – Jehoash	Israel
Micaiah	853	Ahab	Israel
THE 'WRITING' PROPHETS OF THE PERIOD OF THE MONARCHY			
Joel	810 – 750	Joash – Uzziah	Judah
Amos	760	Jeroboam II	Israel
Jonah	760	Jeroboam II	Israel
Hosea	760 – 722	Jeroboam II – Hoshea	Israel
(722: The fall of Samaria)			
Isaiah	740 – 700	Uzziah – Hezekiah	Judah
Micah	740 – 687	Jotham – Hezekiah	Judah
Zephaniah	640 – 610	Josiah	Judah
Nahum	630 – 612	Josiah	Judah
Jeremiah	626 – 580	Josiah – the exile	Judah
Habakkuk	600	Jehoiakim	Judah
(587: The fall of Jerusalem)			
THE 'WRITING' PROPHETS OF THE PERIOD OF THE EXILE			
Daniel	604-535		
Ezekiel	592-570		
Obadiah	? 587		
Haggai	? 520		
Zechariah	? 520		
Malachi	? 450		

Testaments as God's messengers brought his word to bear on the situations in which his people found themselves. There is also a particularly vivid and symbolic type of prophecy known as 'apocalyptic' and this appears in both Old and New Testaments.

The early or 'non-writing' prophets

Moses is the first person in the Bible to be given the title 'prophet', in the sense of being a spokesman for God (Numbers 12:6-8; Deuteronomy 34:10) but it was not until the time of Samuel (c 1060-1000 BC) that the role of prophet became clearly defined. The New Testament speaks of Samuel as the last of the judges and the first of the prophets (Acts 13:20; 3:24).

The 'non-writing' prophets are so called simply because they left no literary legacy. Like the 'writing' prophets who followed them, though, they were the highly significant spiritual, moral and political guides of Israel and Judah. In this earlier period, between the tenth and eighth centuries BC, chief among them were Samuel, Elijah, Elisha and Micaiah. Accounts of their ministries and influence are found in the history books of Samuel, Kings and Chronicles.

They were described in two broad ways:

● **'Man of God':** This was how the prophet would be viewed by the people. He would be noted for his close fellowship with God and for the godliness of his character.

● **'Servant of the Lord':** This describes the relationship of the prophet to God. It is a term used of the prophets by God and by the writers of the narratives in which the prophets feature (see 2 Kings 17:13).

The prophets of this period operated in two main ways:

● **In groups:** Groups of prophets, such as those described in 1 Samuel 10:5-6; 19:19-24, were given to an 'ecstatic' form of prophecy, seeming to be 'taken over' *en masse* by the Spirit of God. They may have been associated with a particular sanctuary where they may have helped provide the music for worship.

Groups of prophets, known as 'sons of the prophets' attached themselves to a significant prophet of their day. There were a group of one hundred prophets who frequently met with Elisha and regarded him as their mentor (2 Kings 4:38-44; 6:1-7). They appear to have spent considerable periods of time living a communal way of life.

In the later history of Israel, groups of paid prophets were employed at the king's court (see, for example, 2 Chronicles 18:5).

● **The lone prophet:** There were several outstanding figures who acted as political and religious guides for the nation. They were often called to bring God's rebuke, warning or encouragement to the kings of Israel and Judah. These men were usually known as 'seers' − those who 'see' the word of God through dreams and visions. An alternative title for them (used also for the groups of prophets) is the Hebrew word *nabi* − simply translated 'prophet' − meaning 'he who calls' or 'he who is called'. Both shades of meaning give an accurate picture of the prophets, as men and women who called people back to obedience to God and as servants of God who had first been called by him to their task.

Martin Luther King, assassinated in 1968, is regarded by many Christians as a modern prophet. He spoke and acted prophetically on a key issue of our times – the oppression of black people in western societies.

The classic or 'writing' prophets

● **Prophets of the monarchy:** Prophets ministering during this period, and whose oracles have been recorded in the books of the Old Testament named after them, are Amos, Jonah, Hosea, Isaiah, Micah, Zephaniah, Nahum, Jeremiah and Habakkuk. Their task was to confront king and commoner alike with the demands of the covenant. Alongside this 'preaching' function the prophets also predicted national calamity if the people persisted in their rebellion against God's laws. Yet they also foresaw that God would provide salvation for a few, a 'remnant' of the people.

● **Prophets of the exile:** The role of the prophets of this period was to explain to the people what had gone wrong and why they were in exile; to show that God was faithful to his covenant though the people were not; and to bring them hope of a new beginning in their own land. These were the prophets Ezekiel, Obadiah, Haggai, Zechariah and Malachi.

New Testament prophets

● **John the Baptist:** The prophetic ministry of John the Baptist broke a silence of four hundred years. There had been no prophetic word from God to his people since the time of Malachi. In the New Testament John the Baptist is seen as a prophet in the same mould as Elijah: his rugged appearance, desert lifestyle and lack of regard for the rulers of the day being strongly reminiscent of Elijah.

Malachi had prophesied that 'Elijah' would return before 'the great and dreadful day of the Lord' (Malachi 4:5-6) and John the Baptist saw himself as the forerunner of the Messiah, preparing the people for his coming (Matthew 3:1-12). Jesus confirmed this, telling the crowds that John was indeed a prophet and that his ministry sealed the end of the old order of prophets and law (Matthew 11:7-15).

● **Jesus:** Jesus himself is regarded as a prophet by the New Testament writers – though not of the same order as the other prophets. The task of the prophets up till the time of Jesus had been to bring the word of God to his people. Jesus was a prophet of a different kind because he *was* the Word of God (John 1:1). There could be no clearer or more full revelation of God than that which appeared in the person of Christ.

THE PROPHET'S ROLE

A prophet like Moses

At the end of Moses' life, God promised that he would raise up 'a prophet like you' from among the people to continue to bring God's word to them: 'I will put my words in his mouth, and he will tell them everything I command him' (see Deuteronomy 18:15-19). So Moses' ministry became the standard by which all future prophetic ministries were measured.

In time the identity of the 'prophet like me' about whom Moses spoke took on greater significance. Many began to believe that in the very last days God would raise up a second 'Moses' to mediate perfectly between God and man. Jesus' actions suggested that he saw himself fulfilling this role (John 6:1-15, 25-59) and the apostles made it plain that Jesus was the ultimate prophet and mediator foretold by Moses (Acts 3:17-26). This was also the view of the writer to the Hebrews (Hebrews 3). Moses was the mediator of the old covenant and brought into being the Jewish kingdom of Israel; Jesus was the mediator of the new covenant and brought into being the worldwide kingdom of God.

Characteristics

The chief characteristics of the prophetic role are all found in the ministry of Moses.

The most important factor was that the prophet should be called into the role by God. No one who set himself up as a prophet was regarded as genuine. Jeremiah, Ezekiel, Amos and Isaiah all tell of their call to the prophetic ministry by God.

> **JEREMIAH**
> The word of the Lord came to me, saying, 'Before I formed you in the womb I knew you, before you were born I set you apart; I appointed you as a prophet to the nations.'

> **AMOS**
> I was neither a prophet nor a prophet's son, but I was a shepherd, and I also took care of sycamore-fig trees. But the Lord took me from tending the flock and said to me, 'Go and prophesy to my people Israel.'

> **EZEKIEL**
> He said to me... 'Son of man, I am sending you to the Israelites... Say to them, "This is what the Sovereign Lord says."'

> **ISAIAH**
> I heard the voice of the Lord saying, 'Whom shall I send? And who will go for us?' And I said, 'Here am I. Send me!' He said, 'Go...'

If evidence of a divine call was a vital part of a prophet's curriculum vitae, the job description he might be given would look something like this:

WANTED!

A PROPHET LIKE MOSES, APPOINTED BY GOD

- To speak God's words
- To remind the people of the demands of God's Law
- To interpret history
- To combine proclamation with prediction
- To confront kings and play an active part in national affairs
- To intercede for God's people in prayer
- To live in close communion with God

● **To speak God's words:** All true prophets recognised that unless they were given God's words they had nothing to say to God's people. So God told Moses: 'I will help you speak and will teach you what to say' (Exodus 4:12).

Jeremiah describes how 'the Lord reached out his hand and touched my mouth and said to me, "Now, I have put my words in your mouth" ' (Jeremiah 1:9). Ezekiel graphically describes the same experience in terms of eating a scroll on which was written God's message for his people (Ezekiel 2:8-3:4).

● **To remind the people of the demands of God's law:** The moral, ethical and religious demands of the law were all bound up together. God's people were to reflect the holiness of God in their worship and the love and justice of God in their relationships with one another. The prophets' task was to call people back to those standards, to goad their consciences until they took action. Amos and Micah in particular launched stinging attacks on those who grew rich at the expense of others and who denied justice to the poor.

> 'Woe to those who plan iniquity,
>   to those who plot evil on their beds!
> At morning's light they carry it out
>   because it is in their power to do it.
> They covet fields and seize them,
>   and houses, and take them.
> They defraud a man of his home,
>   a fellow-man of his inheritance.'
>   (Micah 2:1-2)

The words of the Old Testament prophets about the poor and the hungry speak just as sharply to us today as they did to their original hearers. How will we respond to them?

95

● **To interpret history:** The prophets turned history into revelation by being able to explain why things were happening as they were. Amos, for example, was able to predict the downfall of the city of Gaza, state that its destruction had been ordered by God, and explain why:

'This is what the Lord says:
"For three sins of Gaza,
  even for four, I will not turn back my wrath.
Because she took captive whole communities
  and sold them to Edom,
I will send fire upon the walls of Gaza
  that will consume her fortresses." '
(Amos 1:6-7)

He added, 'Surely the Sovereign Lord does nothing
  without revealing his plan
  to his servants the prophets.'
(Amos 3:7)

● **To combine proclamation with prediction:** The prophets were not simply preachers, proclaiming the demands of God's law. They also predicted future happenings. But they were concerned with the future only in as far as it affected present actions. They would warn of future judgment in order to stress the need for changes in the present. They would tell of God's blessing in the future in order to comfort the demoralised and despairing exiles.

● **To confront kings and play an active part in national affairs:** The monarchs were the most powerful people with which the prophets had to deal. Moses' first task was to confront Pharaoh with the demand for the release of his Hebrew slaves. Samuel confronted Saul over his disobedience to God's instructions (1 Samuel 15:12-29) bringing him the chilling news, 'Because you have rejected the word of the Lord, he has rejected you as king.' Similarly, Nathan confronted David about his adultery and murder (2 Samuel 12:1-14); Elijah confronted Ahab about his disregard for God's laws of inheritance and for his part in the murder of Naboth (1 Kings 21:1-29); Isaiah confronted Hezekiah over his boastful and foolhardy display of the temple treasures to envoys from the king of Babylon (Isaiah 39:1-8).

● **To intercede for God's people in prayer:** The prophets were called to stand in the breach between God and humankind. In the same way that Moses had represented the people before God (Exodus 18:19) and interceded with God on their behalf (Exodus 32:30-35), the later prophets were asked to pray to God on behalf of others (see 2 Kings 19:4, for instance).

● **To live in close communion with God:** The prophets could only know the mind of God if they were living in constant fellowship with him. Alec Motyer writes, 'Prophecy came about as part of the prophet's conscious fellowship with the Lord.' (Alec Motyer, *The Day of the Lion.* Leicester: IVP,1984.) Jeremiah describes a true prophet as one who 'stood in the council of the Lord to see or to hear his word' (Jeremiah 23:18). In addition, as the prophets' task was to call the people back to spiritual purity, they themselves had to live in daily obedience to God. When they did not, they were swiftly removed from the scene (1 Kings 13:1-26). One of the marks of a false prophet was that his prophecies did not come true, but another equally good guide as to whether he should be listened to or not was that of the integrity of his own lifestyle.

THE PROPHETS' MESSAGE

The themes which are usually associated with the prophets come out most clearly in the writings of the eighth-century prophets: Amos, Hosea, Micah, Isaiah.

Israel's God

They spoke of God's character and of the nature of his relationship with his people. He is described as:

► The creator of Israel   (Jeremiah 18:1-10)
   - transcendent, awesome   (Ezekiel 1)

► The father of Israel   (Jeremiah 31:9; Hosea 11:1-4)
   - loving, slow to anger   (Hosea 3:1; 11:8; Nahum 1:3;)

► The redeemer of Israel   (Isaiah 60:16)
   - merciful and forgiving   (Micah 7:18; Isaiah 1:18)

► The Holy One of Israel   (Isaiah 6:1-5; 43:14-15)
   - just and righteous   (Jeremiah 9:24)

Judgment

● **On Israel:** The covenant relationship between God and Israel was likened to a marriage relationship. The relationship was sustained and protected by the laws surrounding it, so when the people began to disregard the laws and to turn away from God the prophets compared their action to adultery (Jeremiah 2-3).

But a 'divorce' of God from his people would leave them utterly defenceless against the brutal and hostile surrounding nations. The prophets warned of this and painted graphic pictures of the way in which God would allow them to be overrun and taken into captivity (Jeremiah 4:5-31).

Through the agony of his own divorce, the prophet Hosea came to a deep understanding of how God's people had destroyed their relationship with God.

● **Of Israel's oppressors:** The prophets warned that injustice, wherever it was found in the world, would be punished. Assyria, Babylonia, Egypt, Syria, Moab, Edom, Philistia and Tyre are all warned of God's impending judgment (Isaiah 13-23; Jeremiah 46-51; Ezekiel 25-32). Entire books are given over to prophecy against other nations. Obadiah, for example, addresses his prophecy to Edom; Jonah is sent by God to Nineveh, the capital of Assyria. God's added purpose in this was to show that he was God of the whole world and that he would remain faithful to his own people, rescuing her from her oppressors.

Future hope

With the message of punishment on Israel's enemies came the hope that Israel would be restored to her own land. The prophets looked forward to:

● **A return to Israel after the exile:** In the middle of his prophecies about the fall of Jerusalem, Isaiah foresaw that God would bring back a 'remnant' of the nation to rebuild the city and the temple. He even named one of his sons 'A remnant shall return' (Isaiah 7:3).

● **The establishing of a new covenant between God and his people:** The prophets recognised that the people of God needed a fundamental change in nature if they were ever to live in loving obedience to him. It was Jeremiah who spoke most plainly of the new covenant:

> 'The time is coming,' declares the Lord,
> 'when I will make a new covenant
> with the house of Israel
> and with the house of Judah.
> It will not be like the covenant
> I made with their forefathers...
> I will put my law in their minds
> and write it on their hearts.'

(Jeremiah 31:31-33)

Linked with the hope of a new covenant was the prediction of a new outpouring of God's Spirit (Joel 2:28-32); the beginnings of hope for a saviour-figure who would be the perfect 'king' of Israel (Isaiah 9:1-7); and anticipation of a final 'day of the Lord' when God would come bringing judgment and salvation and would create 'a new heaven and a new earth' in which his rule would be absolute (Isaiah 65:17-25).

Call to repentance

Central to the prophets' message was the call to repentance. Wholesale turning back to God was the only thing that could save the people from disaster.

Ezekiel's sweeping condemnation on all segments of society shows the extent to which worship and social life had become corrupted:

> 'Again the word of the Lord came to me, "Son of man, say to the land...
>
> There is a conspiracy of her *princes* within her like a roaring lion tearing its prey; they devour people, take treasures and precious things and make many widows within her.
>
> Her *priests* do violence to my law and profane my holy things; they do not

distinguish between the holy and the common; they teach that there is no difference between the unclean and the clean; and they shut their eyes to the keeping of my Sabbaths, so that I am profaned among them.

Her *officials* within her are like wolves tearing their prey; they shed blood and kill people to make unjust gain.

Her *prophets* whitewash these deeds for them by false visions and lying divinations. They say, 'This is what the Sovereign Lord says' – when the Lord has not spoken.

The *people* of the land practise extortion and commit robbery; they oppress the poor and needy and ill-treat the alien, denying them justice." '   (Ezekiel 22:23-29, italics added)

Micah summed up the lifestyle that God demanded from his people instead:

'He has showed you, O man, what is good.
And what does the Lord require of you?
To act justly and to love mercy
and to walk humbly with your God.'

(Micah 6:8)

GETTING THE MESSAGE ACROSS

How did God speak to the prophets?

Often, a prophet would say simply, 'The word of the Lord came to me' and we have no very clear idea of exactly how. The verb 'came' implies, though, 'became actively present'. In other words, the prophet became suddenly aware of God's message. At other times, the prophet would be more specific about how he grasped God's message:

● **Through visions or dreams:** The old word for prophet, 'seer', was an apt one. In Numbers 12:6 God is recorded as saying:

'When a prophet of the Lord is among you,
I reveal myself to him in visions,
I speak to him in dreams.'

Jeremiah sometimes received God's word through dreams (Jeremiah 31:26); and Zechariah, Isaiah and Ezekiel all record vivid revelatory visions (Zechariah 1:7-6:8; Isaiah 6; Ezekiel 1-3:14). Daniel gained a reputation at the court of Nebuchadnezzar for being able to understand what God was saying through the king's dreams (Daniel 2:27-28, 46-47).

● **Through objects and symbols:** Sometimes God would draw the attention of a prophet to an object, which the prophet would then percieve to have a symbolic meaning. Amos, looking at a basket of ripe fruit, suddenly perceived that the sins of Israel had 'ripened'. The nation was ready for 'eating' or destruction (Amos 8:1-2). Jeremiah was at the house of the local potter, watching him mould the clay on the wheel, when he perceived that God was saying he was like the potter and Israel was like the clay. God had the right to do with Israel as he wished (Jeremiah 18:1-11).

● **Through prayer and reflection:** Not all revelation was sudden and 'ecstatic'. On one occasion Jeremiah took several days to think and pray before prophesying (Jeremiah 42). The prophets must also have spent a great deal of time studying the written laws available to them, as they were thoroughly familiar with their demands.

In Ezekiel's most striking vision (in Ezekiel 37), he sees a battlefield covered in the bones of Israel's defeated army. But by God's power, the bones are brought together and the army lives once more. This battlefield is from World War I.

How did they get their messages across?

The prophets were masters of communication; they had to be because their message was usually unpalatable and difficult to accept.

● **Story-telling:** Nathan slid a barbed message into an innocent-sounding story in order to catch King David off guard and make him hear God's rebuke (2 Samuel 12:1-9).

● **Living it out:** Hosea's message about the spiritual adultery of Israel was underscored by the adultery of his own wife. God's command to him was to continue to love her, despite the fact that she had deserted him; to go looking for her and to buy her out of the slavery or prostitution into which she had fallen. That, said God, would be a picture of his love for Israel and would be his call to Israel to return to purity of worship (Hosea 1-3).

● **Drama:** Ezekiel acted out the coming seige of Jerusalem. He survived for many weeks on the barest rations of food, illustrating the famine of a besieged city, then cut off his hair and scattered it around the city with a sword, graphically showing that those people who escaped the attacking army and survived the food shortage would be scattered into distant lands (Ezekiel 4-5).

● **Prophetic action:** As the army of Babylon set up seige ramps against the walls of Jerusalem, it was plain that, to all intents and purposes, life in and around Jerusalem was finished. But Jeremiah's message from God was that his people would one day return to the city. To demonstrate the certainty of this Jeremiah arranged to buy a field from his cousin, telling his scribe to take the deeds of sale, 'and put them in a clay jar so that they will last a long time. For this is what the Lord Almighty, the God of Israel, says: Houses, fields and vineyards will again be bought in this land' (Jeremiah 32:13-14).

● **Poetry and 'oracles':** Large parts of the prophetic books are written as poetic 'oracles' or paint vivid word pictures of the prophets' visions. In either form they are highly memorable and would probably have been written by the prophets themselves or by a close associate (see Jeremiah 36).

● **Written records:** The messages of the prophets always had a wider application than their immediate audience. Amos and Hosea, for example, were called to minister in the northern kingdom, Israel, but were driven back to the south. It was there that their prophecies were preserved and reapplied to the southern kingdom, Judah.

'Messages which were originally preached to a state which had disappeared from the face of history became relevant next door.'
*(John Job, **The Teaching of The Old Testament**. London: Scripture Union, 1984)*

There were four stages in the transmission of the prophecies to other audiences and future generations:

1 The prophets themselves wrote down many of their messages.

2 The disciples of the prophets played a part in the recording and passing on of their oracles. They also noted down biographical information about the prophets' activities.

3 Collators gathered together all the oracles and narratives about each particular prophet and arranged them into anthologies.

4 Editors continued the work of organisation, adding dates and historical information. They also reinterpreted some of the oracles in order to apply them to the particular conditions of their own time. It is these editors who formed the prophetic material into the biblical books which have come down to us.

PERSONALLY SPEAKING
Hunger in Russia

At the huge gathering of evangelists in Manila in 1989, a Russian evangelist reported that there is tremendous hunger for the Scriptures in rural Russia. He recalled a time when he placed many Bibles and New Testaments on a table in one town square. People were grabbing these Scriptures, hugging them and kissing them. Christian magazines were being torn into pages to be distributed throughout the crowd.

There is a hunger for the Word of God in countries where they have tried to cage the lion – but the lion cannot be caged!

(Reported by Tony Dann, Director of Centres' Development, British Youth for Christ.)

FOR GROUPS:

NO CONCERN OF MINE?

SHARE:

What events reported in the news recently have made you angry because of their injustice? How would you want to change those situations?

READ: Isaiah 1:1-20.

EXPLORE:

1 Why was God weary of the Israelites' worship? (Circle the letter(s) closest to the answer.)
  - (a) He didn't like beef.
  - (b) The Israelites didn't wash their hands first.
  - (c) The people's worship was not genuine.
  - (d) Their worship was fine, but their lives were out of step.
  - (e) It all happened too often.
  - (f) They were doing it for themselves, not for God.
  - (g) Other ....

2 Isaiah wanted the people to...
  - (a) Come to worship more often.
  - (b) Show fairness to the underprivileged.
  - (c) Forget all about public worship.
  - (d) Worship at full moon not new moon.
  - (e) Pray with more sincerity.
  - (f) Confess their sins first.
  - (g) Other ....

3 If I had been among the original hearers my reaction would have been:
  - (a) Leave it out Isaiah, I've attended worship twice a week for the last year.
  - (b) Do you know how much that last bullock cost?
  - (c) Right on Isaiah! You tell 'em!
  - (d) I always said religion wasn't all it was cracked up to be.
  - (e) Maybe I shouldn't have trebled the rents.
  - (f) I must get round to see old Mrs Jones this week, she's so lonely.
  - (g) Other ....

4 Much of Leviticus and Deuteronomy describe the various sacrifices that the people should offer. If this was what God had commanded, what was the problem (see verse 10 and onwards)?

5 What did God most want from his people?

6 How would your church take to the news that God cares as much about social justice as correct worship?
 (a) They wouldn't understand the term 'social justice'.
 (b) Horrified.
 (c) Insist that worship and evangelism were all that concerned God.
 (d) Say 'Great!' But do nothing.
 (e) Look at the needs of those around them to see what had to be done.
 (f) Other...

7 On a cold winter morning you are just about to leave for church — in a hurry as usual — when the lady next door (whose husband died last year) calls you. Her fire isn't working and she thinks the fuse has blown. What do you do?
 (a) Skip church and mend the fuse.
 (b) Say you'll look at it later.
 (c) Give her the fuse wire and a screwdriver.
 (d) Point out that the guy two doors down is an electrician.
 (e) Say you don't really know anything about fuses.

8 If God issued the invitation of verse 18 to you, what would you put on the agenda? List them on a piece of paper, then put them together with everyone else's. Now tear up or burn all the lists while someone reads 1 John 1:5-2:2.

9 What situations in your community might be addressed by verse 17? Draw up a detailed, practical plan of action for how you as a group could deal with one of them. Pray together about ways of seeing it through.

(Adapted from John Grayston, **From God With Love**. London: Scripture Union, 1985.)

UNDERSTANDING PROPHETIC LITERATURE

The prophetic books are not the only books of the Bible which deal with God's revelation of his plans. The history books, for instance, also interpret events in the light of God's revealed plans. The prophetic books are grouped together, however, because of their distinctive *style* of revelation. Stephen Motyer, in *Unlock the Bible* (London: Scripture Union, 1990), points to three things that distinguish prophetic revelation from other forms of revelation:

● The prophets always ministered in a crisis. They were God's spokesmen, warning, accusing or giving hope – whatever was appropriate at the time.

● The prophets spoke with a sense of urgency, wanting an immediate response from the people. They were acutely aware of the reality of impending judgment or future restoration and spoke about the future in order to bring about a change in people's actions in the present.

● The prophets used language in an unusual way, piling vivid images on top of each other to create effect and to heighten the sense of urgency in their message.

Besides these factors, a number of different types of literature are found in the prophetic books: oracles, visions, poetry, autobiographical and biographical narrative.

How, then, should we set about understanding and interpreting the message of the prophets?

The prophets spoke in violent, troubled times. This Assyrian king hunted in a war chariot, which was as fearsome in its day as the *Challenger* tank is in ours.

Be aware of the situation

The centuries in which the 'writing' prophets ministered were times of great political, military, social and economic upheaval. God's people lurched from one crisis to another and the prophets brought them God's message for particular times and situations. Which kingdom was the prophet operating in? Or did he prophesy during the exile? What was happening on the international and national scenes? Which king, if any, was the prophet most closely in touch with? This information can be found in commentaries, in the books of Kings and Chronicles and in some of the prophetic books themselves.

Read whole 'oracles'

The prophetic oracles should be read as wholes in order to grasp the thought of the prophet but it is not always easy to work out where an oracle begins and ends. A useful guide is to note the different 'forms' of oracle. Fee and Stuart outline the three major forms in their book *How to read the Bible for all its worth.*

● **The lawsuit:** This is an ancient version of the contemporary courtroom drama. It is an oracle in which God, the plaintiff, brings charges against Israel, the defendant, which detail the ways in which Israel has broken the terms of the covenant. There is a summons, a charge, evidence is given and a verdict is pronounced. God, besides being plaintiff, is also judge. (See, for example, Isaiah 3:13-26.)

● **The woe:** The cry of 'Woe!' signified death or fear to the Israelite. It would be heard at a funeral or in the face of a great disaster. So it was particularly striking when used by the prophets. The 'woe' oracles contain three elements: an announcement of distress, the reason for the distress, a prediction of the disaster that is to come. (See, for example, Micah 2:1-5.)

● **The promise:** The promise or 'salvation oracle' contains three elements: a reference to the future, usually in terms of, 'In that day...'; mention of radical change, and a promise of blessing. (See, for example, Amos 9:11-15; Hosea 2:16-23; Jeremiah 31:1-9.)

Recognise the symbolism

The prophets used symbolism and figurative language a great deal because it conjured up images that stuck in people's minds and continued to work away in them. In Isaiah 29:5-6, for example, Isaiah writes of God coming to the defence of Jerusalem when it has been attacked and destroyed by its enemies: 'Suddenly, in an instant,
the Lord Almighty will come
with thunder and earthquake and with great noise,
with windstorm and tempest and flames of a devouring fire.'
Isaiah did not expect literal thunder, earthquakes, windstorms, tempest and raging fire to accompany the coming deliverance; so it would be wrong to think that he is prophesying some future, world-shattering catastrophe. His language is rather a graphic way of asserting that God is sovereign over the whole of the natural world, just as the designation 'Lord Almighty' indicates that all the armies of heaven and earth are at his disposal. Isaiah's choice of symbolism—thunder, fire and smoke—echoes that used in Exodus 19:16-19 to describe God's 'descent' onto Mount Sinai to give the ten commandments to Moses. Within the prophetic writings, these images became classic symbols of the presence of God, and particularly of his coming in judgment.

UNDERSTANDING
APOCALYPTIC PROPHECY

The apocalyptic books are prophecy in technicolour. As such they have many features in common with the other prophetic writings, but several distinctive elements too.

Daniel and Revelation are the two major apocalyptic works in the Bible, though Ezekiel and the Gospels contain apocalyptic elements (Mark 13, Matthew 24, Luke 21, for example).

Apocalyptic Passages in the Bible:

EZEKIEL	DANIEL	ZECHARIAH
Apocalyptic passages appear throughout Ezekiel – see especially Chapter 1	The second half of Daniel contains apocalyptic visions (chapters 7–12)	Apocalyptic passages are scattered throughout Zechariah's prophecies

MATTHEW MARK & LUKE	2 PETER & JUDE	REVELATION
Jesus uses apocalyptic imagery in speaking about the future (Matt 24; Mark 13; Luke 21)	These two letters are full of apocalyptic pictures, language and warnings	Revelation is *the* apocalyptic book of the Bible

General features

● **Reveals the activity of God:** The term 'apocalyptic' derives from the Greek word for 'revelation'– *apocalypsis*. It is the revealing to God's people of what God is doing, both in the events in which they find themselves and, especially, in the larger scale and longer term.

● **Given in a crisis:** Like the other prophets, the apocalyptic writers had a reason for writing. The literary form was particularly popular between 200 BC and 100 AD, another time of major political and religious upheaval for the Jewish people. When evil seemed to be in control and God appeared to be silent and far-removed from his people, the apocalyptic writers brought a dual message: God is in control of the world despite the apparent triumph of evil; and the days of evil are numbered.

John wrote Revelation for the churches of his day and saw what he wrote as significant for their time – not simply for a time in far-off years.

Because of the amazingly accurate predictions of the book of Daniel, some scholars believe it was written after the events it describes (in about 165 BC rather than about 610 BC). The crisis would be different but Daniel's 'prophecies' would still bring comfort to the Jewish people. The evidence to support this theory is not, however, convincing. In any case, it still has to allow for the genuine nature of the predictions that were fulfilled after 165 BC.

The temple area in modern Jerusalem. Many of the prophets spoke about the coming destruction of Jerusalem's temple, in punishment for the people's sins. The temple became a symbol of God's presence with his people.

● **Highly symbolic:** In apocalyptic writing the prophetic 'word of the Lord' gives way to revelation through visions or dreams. There is therefore a far higher reliance on fantastic, 'other-worldly' imagery to convey the message. The symbolism becomes more highly developed too; numbers, in particular, become very significant.

Reading to understand

● **Note the reason for writing:** The churches to which John wrote were beginning to suffer severe persecution. John himself was a prisoner on Patmos. He writes to give his fellow-Christians courage to face ongoing persecution and also to assure them that their eventual salvation and God's final judgment on evil are certain.

Daniel received his 'revelation' in exile in Babylon. The people of God were scattered and totally demoralised. Their question was, 'How can we sing the songs of the Lord while in a foreign land?' (Psalm 137:4.) In other words, 'Where is God now?' Daniel's apocalypse answered this: God knows where his people are: past, present and future; and the future triumph of God's plan for his people is certain.

The Book of Revelation was written partly to encourage Christians suffering severe persecution. Its powerful images have brought hope to many people in the suffering church. This photograph shows Labour Camp 36 at Kuchino in the USSR.

● **Note the setting:** One of the biggest pitfalls in reading the apocalyptic books is to fail to notice where the action takes place. Are the events described happening on earth or in heaven? John's visions in Revelation are largely concerned with showing what is happening, or what will happen, in 'heaven' – the spiritual realm – rather than on earth. What he sees going on there does of course affect people on earth, but should not automatically be equated with events on earth.

● **Be aware of the symbolism:** Because symbolism is such an important feature of apocalyptic writing it needs careful handling. The following points should be remembered:

► The symbols should be understood with the imagination rather than with logic and detailed analysis. They are presented to us like a giant picture book; we should *see* what is happening before we begin to interpret it.

► The symbols are only pictures of reality. They do not necessarily describe exactly how things will be. We should not assume, for instance, that the plagues heralded by the trumpet blasts and which devastate the earth are scientific descriptions of such things as defoliation, pollution of the sea and nuclear holocaust. John's message may be a more 'theological' one, assuring his readers that, as with the plagues on Egypt, God's concern will not be to destroy people but to bring them to repentance.

▶ Sometimes the visionary himself will interpret the symbols. For example, John intends his readers to understand that the person he describes as 'like a son of man' (Revelation 1:13) is Jesus, the one who was dead but who now lives for ever (1:18). In the same way he explains that the 'prostitute' of chapter 17 is the 'great city' of chapter 18 (see 17:5).

▶ Note the significance of numbers. Numbers are very important both to Daniel and John, but are rarely meant literally. Threes, sevens and their sum, tens, are symbolic of perfection and completeness. They symbolise the work of God. Six, on the other hand, is imperfection – symbolising the work of man or of the enemies of God.

▶ Look for the main point of the symbol. The way John describes the 'beast' that emerges from the sea (Revelation 3:1-10) reveals that it is a counterfeit of Christ, demanding the worship due to God alone. John's main point is pastoral: the present persecution of the Christians originates with the Devil, who is using the Roman emperor as his agent. To give in to the emperor's demands to denounce Christ and to worship him instead is in fact to agree to worship the Devil. In the light of this, John calls his readers to 'patient endurance and faithfulness' (13:10). The details themselves – the ten horns, blasphemous names, head wound, etc – do not call for individual interpretation. They are not the message, merely means of conveying what actually is John's message.

ISSUES IN REVELATION

Ways of interpreting Revelation

Revelation has been interpreted in many different ways. There are basically four approaches to undertanding it.

● **The whole sweep of history:** On this view, Revelation sets out the whole panorama of history from the first century until the end of time. It is basically a presentation of the events of those years.

● **A 'tract for the times':** This roots the book firmly in the events of the writer's own day. It is seen as a 'tract for the times', explaining the meaning of events happening in the first century, and not attempting to look into the future.

● **A glimpse of the future:** By contrast, this view maintains that from chapter 4 onwards Revelation deals only with the events surrounding the second coming of Jesus. People who adopt this position usually also hold a premillennialist view (see below).

● **The symbolic view:** This maintains that Revelation is a collection of symbolic pictures of such timeless truths as the victory of good over evil. These are not meant to be understood in any historical way, but are meant to encourage persecuted Christians with the knowledge that God will ultimately triumph over all that is evil.

Each of these views contains an element of truth. Each taken on its own, however, tends to give a distorted message.

It is probably best to combine elements of all four views. It is true that Revelation does give a panoramic, impressionistic view of church history, as the historist view maintains. It is also rooted firmly in the circumstances of the first century; John's concern was a pastoral one and the persecution he witnessed around him prompted him to write. At the same time we cannot deny that the book speaks of the end of time and the return of Christ. The symbolic language of Revelation gives a graphic picture of reality, challenging the Christian to continue to witness to Christ even when the opposition is fierce, and bringing him or her the assurance that God will ultimately judge and destroy all evil.

The millennium

Many civilized discussions between Christians have turned into heated and confused arguments when the subject of the millennium is raised. What is it all about?

The word 'millennium' derives from the Latin for 'thousand'. It refers to the 'thousand year' rule of Christ mentioned in Revelation 20:4. It is preceded by the 'binding' of Satan:

'And I saw an angel coming down out of heaven, having the key to the Abyss and holding in his hand a great chain. He seized the dragon, that ancient serpent, who is the devil, or Satan, and bound him for a thousand years. He threw him into the Abyss, and locked and sealed it over him, to keep him from deceiving the nations any more until the thousand years were ended...

I saw thrones on which were seated those who had been given authority to judge. And I saw the souls of those who had been beheaded because of their testimony for Jesus and because of the word of God. They had not worshipped the beast or his image and had not received his mark on their foreheads or their hands. They came to life and reigned with Christ a thousand years...'

(Revelation 20:1-4)

After this, Satan is released again and gathers together the armies of the earth to make war on God's people. God then steps in to destroy Satan and the armies and the next scene to be described is the day of judgment, with all people gathered before God's judgment throne. Those who are not the Lord's are thrown into 'the lake of fire'; those who are the Lord's are next pictured in the new Jerusalem.

This thousand-year period and the events surrounding it, have been interpreted in three main ways.

● **Premillennialism (Christ returns before the millennium):** Those who hold this view believe that Jesus will return after a time of war, famine, earthquakes, great apostasy, the appearance of the Antichrist, and a time of

tribulation. Jesus will then reign on earth in person for one thousand years. Evil will be held in check as the covenant promises are fulfilled. This will be followed by a great rebellion and the last judgement. Some premillennialists prefer to see the 'thousand' as symbolic of the perfect quality of the time rather than its extent.

There are two forms of premillennialism:

▶ Historic premillennialism. This is the older of the two views and was the main view of the end times during first three centuries of the Christian era. With the conversion of the emperor Constantine the amillennial view (see below) gained favour until in 431 at the Council of Ephesus, premillennialism was actually condemned as being 'superstitious'. In the Middle Ages, however, it again became popular among 'breakaway' groups of Christians who could no longer identify the corrupt offical church with the people of God. Instead, they began to view the offical church as Satanic and the Pope as the Antichrist.

▶ Dispensational premillennialism. This type of premillennialism developed under the teaching of John Darby (1800-1882) in Britain, who founded the Plymouth Brethren, and Cyrus Scofield (1843-1921) in America, who incorporated Darby's teaching into the notes of his *Reference Bible*. They lived in the wake of the French Revolution, which seemed to mark the beginning of the end. For instance, as a result of the Revolution, anti-Christian beliefs were being openly promulgated for the first time since Constantine.

Darby and Scofield believed that God acted in history in terms of dispensations – periods of time in which different groups of people are required to respond to God according to the way in which he has revealed himself to them. Israel, in particular, was held to relate to God under a different dispensation than the church. The promises made to her under the old covenant, therefore – relating to her inheritance of the land in particular – were not thought to have been revoked under the new covenant. Old and new covenants operate side by side. Dispensationalists today therefore believe that the physical nation of Israel will play an important part in the events of the end times. Some see the thousand-year rule of Revelation 20 entirely in terms of a restored national Israel, with Christ at its head.

The premillenialist view is held by the majority of evangelicals in America today. Those who are also dispensationalists are almost inevitably bound to be supporters of modern Zionism too.

● **Postmillennialism (Christ returns after the millennium):** Those who hold this view suggest that the events of chapter 19 do not refer to the second coming. Rather, they are thought to describe symbolically the way the church, under Christ's lordship, will win the rest of the world for Christ. Once this has been done, Christ will return (chapter 20). He will raise the dead, judge and bind Satan and his followers, and bring into being the new heaven and new earth.

Not many people in Europe or the United States hold to this view today. It was particularly characteristic of the Puritan tradition in seventeenth-century England, and rose to prominence again in the nineteenth century. During this latter period there was every evidence that the church was on its way to evangelising the world. Missionary work was flourishing and it seemed obvious that the civilized, technologically advanced European way of life was bringing about the Utopia of the millennium. Hopes of this were pretty thoroughly squashed, however, by the major catastrophes of the first and second World Wars. It is in the two-thirds world that the postmillennial view is now gaining in popularity.

● **Amillennialism (There is no millennium):** This view sees chapter 20 as a recapitulation of all that has gone so far. There is no specific period during which Christ is seen to rule. The thousand years are viewed symbolically: Satan was bound by Jesus (Mark 3:27; Luke 10:18), though is not yet finally destroyed, and the reign of the saints began with Jesus' ascension to the Father (Ephesians 2:6). The first resurrection is taken to mean conversion, and the second refers to vindication at the day of judgment.

Amillennialism has been the view of many Christians since the time of Augustine, and is probably held by the majority of churches in England today.

ISRAEL AND THE FULFILMENT OF PROPHECY

Many Christians, especially those who hold a dispensational view of God's activity in the world (see above) keep an eye on the news to see what is happening to Israel. Many prophecies in the Bible seem to indicate that the return of the Jews to Israel will herald the last days and that, before the return of Christ, there will be a mass turning to Christ of the Jewish people. Others believe that the people of God are no longer the Jews, but the church, and that the Jews as a nation have no further part to play in the plan of God.

Soldiers on patrol in Israel. Some Christians see the state of Israel, which came into existence in 1948, as the fulfilment of many Old Testament prophecies.

Questions about the role of Israel in God's plan for the world are not new. They were burning issues in the first Christian community in Rome, which was made up of large numbers of Jews as well as Gentiles. Paul wrote a letter to them addressing their questions. At the end of Romans 9–11, the closely argued section at the heart of his teaching, he concludes: 'So all Israel will be saved' (Romans 11:26).

Paul seems to imply that once 'the full number of the Gentiles has come in' there will be a turning again of Israel to God. This is because 'God's gifts and his call are irrevocable' and because his grace extends to the disobedient and the sinner — Jew and Gentile alike. This sounds straightforward enough, but three vital questions remain: Who does Paul mean by 'Israel'? What does he mean by 'all'? On what terms are they saved?

Who does Paul mean by Israel?

Paul uses the term 'Israel' in two ways in Romans. For example, in 9:6 he says, 'not all who are descended from Israel are Israel'. So when he says, 'all Israel will be saved' does he mean all physical Israel? Or does he mean all 'the elect' – the 'true Israel of God'? Commentators are divided over this but many believe that the latter interpretation best fits the thrust of Paul's argument throughout the rest of the letter.

Paul's argument is that the Israelite people have always been the people of the Messiah, 'according to the flesh'. That is, they are the people from whom the Messiah came, and for whom he came. Yet they killed him. And, because their Messiah has died they can no longer be his people 'according to the flesh'. Physical Israel has died with its Messiah. Some will become the people of God again when they come back to God through faith in the risen Christ.

What does he mean by 'all'?

A number of suggestions have been made about this.

● **All physical Israel:** Some maintain that Paul believed all Israelites who have ever lived will be saved. But if the 'all' here is taken to mean this, the 'all' a little further on in the passage (verse 32) must be taken literally too. In verse 32 he says, 'God has bound all men over to disobedience so that he may have mercy on them all.' The statement parallels that in Romans 5:18: 'Just as the result of one trespass was condemnation for all men, so also the result of one act of righteousness was justification that brings life for all men.'

In each of these verses is Paul using the word 'all' in two different senses or did he really teach that everyone would be saved in the end? It would seem odd for Paul to express great grief at the prospect of many of his fellow Jews not being saved (9:3) if, in fact, he believed they would be. The belief that everyone will eventually be saved (universalism) also seems to make a nonsense of the prophets' passionate pleas to Israel to turn back to God, and of Jesus' graphic warnings to repent before it was too late.

● **All Jews of the last generation:** Many commentators favour the view that there will be a huge revival among the Jews just before the return of Christ. But this view has its problems too.

On what basis does God still regard physical Israel as 'my people'? He can only regard them this way if the old covenant is still in operation, in parallel with the new covenant. God relates to Gentiles through the new covenant (those who respond become 'the church') but continues to relate to the Jews through the old covenant.

The necessary and unsatisfactory conclusion of this line of thinking is that the Jews are saved by a means other than the death of Christ.

● **All elect Israelites:** This is the only interpretation which fits the rest of Paul's teaching in Romans. It is all 'true' Israel who will be saved. Stephen Motyer defines them as 'the entire company of those "from the Jews" whom God wills to call "my people", in fulfilment of his purposes of election.' (Stephen Motyer, **Israel in the plan of God**. Leicester: IVP, 1989.)

On what terms are they saved?

We can see, then, that Jews will be saved on exactly the same terms as Gentiles. The Jews do still feature in God's plan for the world in that the promises of the covenant are still offered to them. Everything that was

Paul in the Book of Romans compares the Jewish people to an olive tree. Although the Gentiles have been grafted into the tree and have taken over its life, the Jews could be grafted back in if they accepted the gospel.

promised to them under the old covenant is available to them through Christ in the new covenant. But the promises have been fulfilled in a spiritual way not a physical way. When Christ returns, they, along with the rest of God's people will inherit not just 'the land' of Israel but a new heaven and a new earth. They, along with the rest of God's people will worship in a new temple - the presence of the Lord himself. And they will enjoy these blessings not because they share a national identity but because, with the rest of God's people, they share in his Holy Spirit through faith in Jesus.

PROPHECY IN THE NEW TESTAMENT CHURCH

The New Testament's accounts of the early church, along with the teaching of Paul, show that prophecy was a significant feature in the life of God's people. In some respects it is a very different sort of prophecy from that encountered in the Old Testament. In other ways it is very much the same.

Many churches have rediscovered the gift of prophecy, used in worship. Paul described this gift: 'the one who proclaims God's message speaks to people and gives them help, encouragement and comfort.'

Discontinuity

● After the apostolic era there are no more prophets exactly like those of the Old Testament. They spoke the words of God to his people; Jesus *is* the word of God. No fuller revelation of God's will or character could be given than that given in Christ. The writer to the Hebrews says: 'In the past God spoke to our forefathers through the prophets at many times and in various ways, but in these last days he has spoken to us by his Son' (Hebrews 1:1-2).

● One type of New Testament prophecy is the authoritative word of God, spoken (or written) by the apostles and preserved as scripture, relevant and applicable for all generations. Subsequent prophecies are of a different order and so should not be accorded the same degree of authority as these. On the contrary, the Bible's teaching is the yardstick by which all contemporary prophecy is to be tested. The apostles wrote under the special guidance of the Holy Spirit and were to some extent aware of the significance of their work (see 2 Peter 3:15-16; Revelation 22:18-19).

● In the New Testament the authoritative role passes from that of the prophet to that of the pastor, teacher and elder. Initially, of course, these roles were filled by the apostles themselves.

● The Old Testament prophets spoke in a national context, addressing either Israel or Judah, as God's people, or bringing the message of Israel's God to one of the surounding nations. The New Testament people of God, however, cuts across all national and racial boundaries. So we find that prophecies in the New Testament are not directed to any one nation. The boundary lines are drawn differently: prophecies are directed either to those within the church or to those outside it.

Continuity

● The gift of prophecy was evident in the early church. Paul taught that those who prophesied were enabled to do so by the Holy Spirit. It is probable that the gift of prophecy was given to individuals, at the will of the Holy Spirit, as and when the gift was needed. The purpose of their prophesying was 'to prepare God's people for works of service so that the body of Christ may be built up' (Ephesians 4:11-12).

● Some people were recognised to have special prophetic gifts. Agabus, for example, had the ability to predict the future and was able to warn Paul that imprisonment lay ahead of him in Jerusalem (Acts 21:11). Philip had four daughters with recognised prophetic gifts (Acts 21:8-9).

● As with some Old Testament prophecies, some New Testament ones were given for a particular occasion and did not have lasting significance. In the New Testament we find that the role of the prophets who brought these was to give encouragement, enlightenment or information, rather than moral and ethical instruction; and what they said was to be carefully weighed (1 Thessalonians 5:19-21).

PROPHECY IN THE CHURCH TODAY

Prophecy today?

Joel predicted a time when God would pour out his Spirit on all people:
'Your sons and daughters will prophesy,
    your old men will dream dreams,
    your young men will see visions.
Even on my servants, both men and women,
    I will pour out my Spirit in those days.'
(Joel 2:28-29)
In his Pentecost sermon, Peter announced that 'those days' had arrived (Acts 2:14-18). Some biblical scholars have maintained that the spiritual gifts shown in the early church, as a result of this outpouring of the Spirit, were given only for that period. This belief stems partly from 1 Corinthians 13:8-10, where Paul says that prophecy will cease 'when the perfect comes'. Those who believe the gifts ceased in the first century take the verse to mean 'when all the canonical books of the Bible have been written'. But the majority of commentators believe the verse refers to the 'face-to-face' knowledge of the risen Lord that we shall have when he returns. It is true, however, that the Bible rarely speaks of miracles happening. When they do happen, it seems that they 'cluster' around key points in the story of salvation, such as the exodus, Jesus' ministry, the giving of the Spirit. This has led some to conclude

that the miracles and gifts spoken about in Acts and the New Testament letters were given only to mark the beginning of the church age.

As the institutional church developed there does seem to have been a dying down of prophecy, though spiritual gifts have been manifested throughout the church's history at different times and in different parts of the world. Since the 1960s the 'charismatic movement' in the United States and Britain has emphasised the need to recover the prophetic ministry of the early church. In this it follows the earlier example of the Pentecostal church. It is certainly difficult to deny that spiritual gifts – including that of prophecy – are being used today in many churches to the glory of God and the upbuilding of his people.

Prophecy in the church

The voice of prophecy is heard in the church today in three main ways:

● **The general witness of the church:** The people of God today are God's heralds; it is through the church that God makes himself known to the world. Just as the Father sent Jesus into the world, so Jesus, Lord of the church and Word of God, sends his people into the world. The church's task is to witness to the work of God in Christ, and to witness to the ethical and moral demands of God on all people, as revealed in the Bible.

'When I give food to the poor, they call me a saint. When I ask why the poor have no food, they call me a communist.' *(Dom Helder Camara)*

The prophets showed that God cares passionately about how a society treats its poor and hungry. This concern is always reflected in authentic prophecy.

Prophecy takes to the streets. *March for Jesus* believes in proclaiming the Christian good news publicly, where people can see and hear the message for themselves.

● **A word for the church:** It seems that the Holy Spirit speaks to the church as a whole, internationally and nationally, seeking to move it on in an area of its understanding or action.

▶ Giving new direction. Christians often come together on a large scale today to seek direction from God on such things as world evangelism (the Lausanne Congresses, for example), the role of women in church ministry, and the issues of church unity.

▶ Giving new understanding. Prophecy never contradicts the teaching of the Bible but it may be that a prophetic word calls the church back to a fresh study and appraisal of its understanding of the Bible. This is what happened with Peter. Contrary to what he had understood the Old Testament scriptures to teach, the Holy Spirit showed him that Gentiles too could receive God's Spirit (Acts 10). In recent years, the rich churches of the West have begun to wake up to God's concern for the poor.

▶ Giving new forms of worship. Prophecy was sometimes in evidence in the early church as 'spiritual songs' or hymns of praise to God (Ephesians 5:18-20; Colossians 3:16; 1 Corinthians 14:26). In our day, many new 'spiritual songs' are being written for the people of God, apparently at the prompting of the Holy Spirit. In the form of song, prophecy expresses not only the word of God to his people but also the response of his people to God and his word.

● Personal revelation:

► The pastor or teacher: A pastor or teacher speaks prophetically when he or she brings 'home' to the listener the message of the Bible.

► The member of the church fellowship: An individual may speak prophetically when he or she speaks to another with a special word of encouragement or guidance (1 Corinthians 14:3-5).

► The praying group: When a group of Christians meets together to study the Bible or to seek God's will on a particular issue, a member of the group may speak prophetically as he or she contributes, giving carefully considered guidance, direction or advice.

The Bible's chief aim is to turn us round to face the living God.

Testing prophecy today

Paul, while encouraging his readers to ask God for the gift of prophecy, also insists that they should test anything that purports to be prophecy (1 Thessalonians 5:19 – 21). What should these tests be?

● A genuine prophecy will be intelligible and capable of being judged. In other words, the prophet will not speak incoherently, out of an 'uncontrollable', ecstatic frenzy (1 Corinthians 14:32 – 33).

● A genuine prophecy will be compatible with the Bible's teaching. God will not contradict himself.

'The opposite of false prophecy is not no prophecy, but carefully weighed and tested prophecy.'
(Clive Calver)

● A genuine prophecy will glorify Christ (John 16:14 – 15; 1 Corinthians 12:2 – 3).

● A genuine prophecy will build up or 'edify' the church (1 Corinthians 14:3 – 4).

● A genuine prophecy will be given from a motive of love and will be delivered in a loving way (1 Corinthians 12:31 – 13:3).

The message that claims to be prophetic is to be tested against these standards by those given authority to do so in the church, generally the pastor, elders or teachers (1 Corinthians 14:29).

'Thus says the Lord...'?

Prophecy has often got itself a bad press because of those who are over-zealous rather than accurate in their listening to God. The phrase, 'Thus says the Lord ...' or 'This is what I, the Lord, say ...' is often used to introduce a 'prophetic word from the Lord'. It was used by the Old Testament prophets but we only have one record of this form of words being used in New Testament prophecy – and that was from a prophet whose advice Paul chose not to take (Acts 21:11).

It poses problems for the church fellowship, however, because it 'severely complicates the duty of weighing and discerning the truth of the prophetic words, by clothing the message in a form which seems to claim a divine authority which, if it is such, puts the words outside the area of discussion.' (David Atkinson, *Prophecy*. Grove Booklet on Ministry and Worship, No 49.) There is no need to introduce a message from God in this way. 'The message can be given in less elevated language... This is not to doubt the sincerity of the speaker, but it does impose less of a strain upon those who have the scriptural duty of judging the amount of divine inspiration involved.' (D Gee, **Spiritual Gifts in the Work of Ministry Today.** Missouri: 1963)

FOR GROUPS:

KEEP WATCH!

SHARE:

What is it that you like about the run-up to Christmas? What are the things that you find a chore and a bore as Christmas gets nearer?

READ: Mark 13:1-37.

What if Christmas never came? To many of us the second coming of Jesus may seem like a Christmas that never comes. In this passage, Jesus answers some questions about the future, both near and far off, but above all he encourages an attitude that we all need to develop.

EXPLORE:

1 Why do you think so many of us have a fascination with the future?

2 From the context, what are Peter, James, John and Andrew asking about in verse 4?

3 Jesus doesn't seem to answer their question directly, at least not at first. What is he concerned about?

4 How would Jesus' warnings and encouragement (v 5-13) have helped the disciples in the early years of the church?

5 What relevance do these warnings and encouragements have for us today?

6 Christians have sometimes disagreed about how to interpret Jesus' words in verses 14-23. Some think Jesus is talking about the destruction of the temple in AD 70 and the events leading up to that. Others think these events are still future. Perhaps both views are correct. What evidence is there to support each view?

7 How is the distress described in verses 24-27 different from that described in verses 5-23?

8 Six times Jesus warns his disciples to 'watch, be on guard.' Why? How does this differ from making predictions about exactly when Jesus will return?

9 In what practical ways can we be alert for Jesus' return?

(Adapted from James Hoover, **Mark: Follow Me**. London: Scripture Union, 1986.)

Best buys on the Bible

GENERAL BOOKS
From 'very straightforward' to 'more complex':
Simon Jenkins, *The Bible from scratch*. Tring: Lion Publishing, 1986.
Stephen Motyer, *Unlock the Bible*. London: Scripture Union, 1990.
Christopher Wright, *User's guide to the Bible*. Tring: Lion, 1984.
Gordon Fee and Douglas Stuart, *How to read the Bible for all its worth*. London: Scripture Union, 1983.
John Drane, *Introducing the Old Testament*. Tring: Lion Publishing, 1987.
John Drane, *Introducing the New Testament*. Tring: Lion Publishing, 1986.

DOCTRINE
Reasonably basic introductions:
Robin Keeley (ed), *The Lion handbook of Christian belief*. Tring: Lion, 1982.
C S Lewis, *Mere Christianity*. London: Fontana, 1970.
For those who want more detail:
Leon Morris, *New Testament theology*. Grand Rapids: Zondervan, 1986.
Willem VanGemeren, *The progress of redemption*. Grand Rapids: Zondervan, 1988.

HISTORY
Old Testament:
F F Bruce, *Israel and the Nations*. Exeter: Paternoster Press, 1963.
Eugene Merrill, *A Kingdom of priests*. Grand Rapids: Baker, 1987.
New Testament:
F F Bruce, *New Testament History*. London: Pickering and Inglis, 1982.

GOSPELS
Introductions and interpretation:
John Drane, *Jesus and the four Gospels*. Tring: Lion, 1979.
R T France, *The man they crucified*. Leicester: IVP, 1975.
Joel Green, *How to read the Gospels and Acts*. Leicester: IVP, 1987.
Robert H Stein, *Difficult passages in the Gospels*. Grand Rapids: Baker, 1984; and *Difficult sayings in the Gospels*. Grand Rapids: Baker, 1985.

PROPHECY
Joel Green, *How to read prophecy*. Leicester: IVP, 1986.
For particular subject areas:
Stephen Motyer, *Israel in the plan of God*. Leicester: IVP, 1989.
Robert G Clouse (ed): *The meaning of the millennium: Four views*. Illinois: IVP, 1977.

VIDEO ORDER FORM

The video, *Uncage The Lion*, that accompanies the group Bible study material in this book should be available through your local Christian book shop. Many Christian book shops also run a library system for the hire of videos. If, however, you are unable to obtain a copy of the video through these channels, use this form to order it direct from Scripture Union.

---- ✂ ----

Order:
Please send me *Uncage The Lion* video
for: purchase @ £24.95

      hire   @ £5.00 per week
            from (date) _____ to (date) _____

Please add £1.25 to your cheque or postal order to cover postage and handling costs:

Total of cheque/postal order enclosed with this order:
(Make cheques payable to *Scripture Union Mail Order*)

Cost:

£

£

£ 1.25

£

Your name:_____

Your address:_____

_____

_____

_____ Postcode_____

Post to:
Scripture Union Mail Order, PO Box 38, Bristol BS99 7NA.

Full details of video hire and purchase in Australia and New Zealand may be obtained from Scripture Union, 241 Flinders Lane, Melbourne 3000, Australia and PO Box 760, Wellington, New Zealand.